Then & Now

Cottages and Castles of Maumee

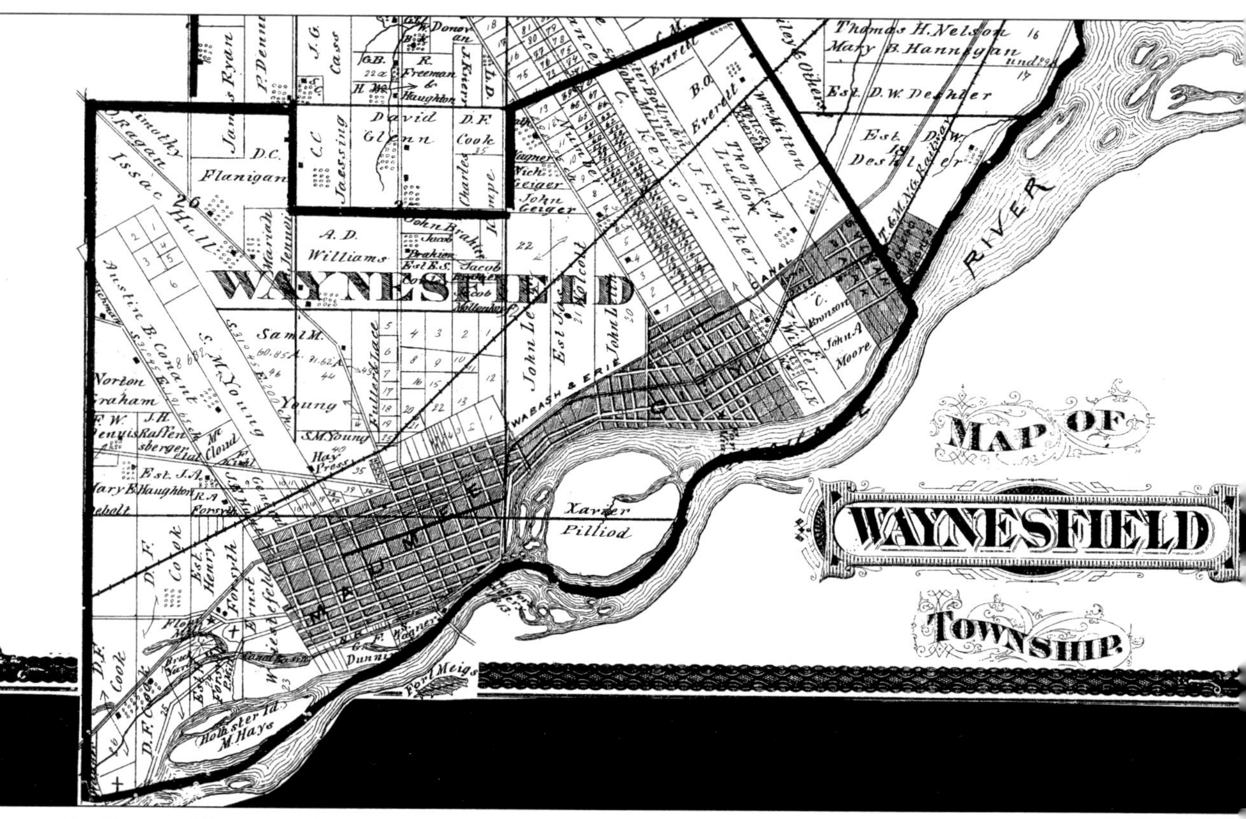

An Early Map of Maumee.

THEN & NOW

COTTAGES AND CASTLES OF MAUMEE

Marilyn Van Voorhis Wendler

ISBN 978-0-7385-1976-0

Published by Arcadia Publishing
Charleston, South Carolina

Printed in the United States of America

Library of Congress Catalog Card Number: 2002105031

For all general information contact Arcadia Publishing at:
Telephone 843-853-2070
Fax 843-853-0044
E-mail sales@arcadiapublishing.com
For customer service and orders:
Toll-Free 1-888-313-2665

Visit us on the Internet at www.arcadiapublishing.com

W. Harrison Street, 1905, Looking East. Pictured, from left to right, are the following: the Richardson/Day House, the Waite House, the Indian Elm, and the Pomeroy House.

Contents

W. HARRISON STREET, 2002. The Waite House is pictured on the left and the Pomeroy on the right.

Introduction

The pioneer architectural historian, I.T. Fray, observed that "whatever monuments people leave behind, none give such intimate and accurate evidence of their character as do the homes in which they lived." The city of Maumee, Ohio, is indeed fortunate that a sizeable number of structures remain to provide testimony to the rich heritage of this Maumee Valley river town. The oldest structures date back to the 1820s and early-1830s. They serve as a reminder of those visionary settlers who brought civilization to the wilderness and whose lives and homes reflected the increased importance of the river trade. Following classical but sturdy forms, the earliest builders constructed their homes in the tradition of the Federal period, with which they were most familiar.

A larger group of houses and structures represent the second rush of Eastern entrepreneurs drawn by the promise of prosperity to come with the completion of the Wabash and Erie Canal. They arrived in the mid-1830s, at the height of the speculative "mania" surrounding the buying and selling of what were known as "wild (canal) lands" and "wild (city) lots"—a reference to the rapid rise and fall in value, rather than the remoteness of location. Confident and optimistic about the future prospects of their city, these pioneering "town builders" borrowed elements of the ancient Greek temples and constructed their homes in Midwestern variations of the American Greek Revival style enjoying popularity back in the East.

While emigrants poured into the river valley, local carpenters were hard pressed to keep up with the demand for new housing. As early as 1832, a Maumee resident observed that "the business of carpentry is brisk around here this season." Five years later, another estimated that the number of buildings going up was about one per day, prompting the *Maumee Express* to implore: "Come on all you carpenters and joiners—our city can give you employment!" Over 150 years later, the remaining examples from that period bear proof to the skill and craftsmanship of those early builders. The "House of Four Pillars" on Maumee's East Broadway, with its pedimented front gable and four fluted columns facing the street, is the city's best-known prototype of the Greek Revival style. However, many more modest examples can be found throughout Maumee's architectural district, identifiable by their distinct Greek Revival details: wide frieze boards returning on the gable end, doorways with sidelights and transoms, symmetrical six-over-six paned windows, and reeded pilasters resembling Greek columns.

Although Greek Revival would continue to be an important architectural influence during the ante-bellum period, a more transitional style evolved as builders adopted the classical elements to the indigenous materials and colloquial preferences of the Midwest. Meanwhile, the introduction of the "balloon frame" greatly simplified the building process, making it possible for any itinerant builder to construct a building to his own specifications without the assistance of a skilled architect. In addition to this vernacular form, the advent of the industrial age facilitated new fashions in architecture, most notably, the Gothic Revival, or American Gothic. It is sometimes referred to as "Carpenter Gothic" because the elaborate scrolling and bracketing which became its hallmarks, could be easily copied from a builder's pattern book by local artisans. By the time of the Civil War, many dignified Greek Revival homes were hidden under machine-made "millwork" with Italianate cornices and jigsaw "curlicues," or modernized with Romanesque turrets and roof, thus complicating the process of identification for later generations.

The mid-to-late Victorian period (1860–1900) introduced a plethora of architectural variations and excesses inspired by the new class of American millionaires. These "Second Empire" homes featured mansard roofs, two-story bays, and heavily-carved lintels. Elaborate porches and porticoes adorned even the simplest frame dwelling and landscaping gained increased importance now that residents had more time to spend enjoying, rather than conquering, nature.

The elaborate ornamentation of the Victorian era began to lose favor toward the end of the 19th century as more and more residents aspired to home ownership. A more modest and affordable design was the story-and-a-half frame house, sometimes referred to as a "country cottage," which was, according to one landlord, the "nearest approach to an ideal neat, cozy, tasty cottage home" for the cost. What these simple frame homes lacked in ostentatious architectural detail was often made up in choice of contrasting exterior colors for window surrounds, bands, cross pieces, and shingled roofs. To complete the effect, a porch or veranda, perhaps trimmed with a touch of Victorian gingerbread, was an important element in a town like Maumee, where "porch sitting" was not only an accepted form of entertainment, but essential to neighborly communication.

The prosperity of the early 20th century and the burgeoning middle class gave rise to a totally new architectural phenomenon—the American Four Square. The Four Square was what the name implies, a square box. The no-nonsense exterior was a modern departure from everything Victorian and it could be adapted to virtually every type of building material and architectural style. It was commonly topped off with a hipped roof and extra space could be gained with the addition of dormers. Its versatility and ease of maintenance made it popular in towns like Maumee which, due to the interurban and other early-20th century transportation innovations, were fast becoming "bedroom communities."

The 20th century also brought a renaissance of earlier styles such as Colonial Revival and English Revival. The Arts and Crafts movement resulted in a house with simple, flowing lines, emphasizing natural woods and a tie with the environment. The bungalow, the first cousin of the cottage, imported from California and warmer climates, also found its way to Maumee. It was particularly popular in the World War I era. But the most revolutionary innovation in the building industry was the introduction of the pre-cut or mail order house, pre-curser of prefabricated buildings. Thousands of these homes were purchased from such companies a Sears, Wards, or the Aladdin Home Company. The pre-cut houses shortened construction time and could be erected by a local builder or even by the home owner. They were especially attractive to small town Midwesterners who could now choose from a variety of designs and by-pass the high labor costs.

The author's goal is not to provide a definitive listing of every 19th-century and early-20th-century home, but to present a representative sample. An attempt was made to establish an approximate construction date based on existing records, family oral history, architectural characteristics and other available historical sources such as local newspapers. A glossary is included to encourage the reader to appreciate the unique qualities of each architectural period and aid in identifying other worthy structures throughout the community. "NRHP" designates homes listed on the National Register of Historic Places.

Chapter 1

1825–1835

"...These are not insignificant huts...but substantial brick and frame edifices, and many of them of a large size..."

Maumee Express, 1837

The editor of the *Express* referred to new homes under construction in 1837, but the following homes, built a decade earlier, were hardly "insignificant" or "huts"! Robert Forsyth and John Hunt traveled from Detroit in 1816 to build a log trading house and a two-story "boarding house." They soon expanded into the wholesaling/forwarding business. Both took an active part in the fledgling community. Forsyth would become the first mayor of Maumee in 1838 and Hunt followed two years later. By 1826, they had abandoned their log structures and, transporting their lumber to and from the Leaming sawmill by ox cart, they built identical homes, side by side. The new homes overlooked the Maumee River and were similar to the styles prevalent in the East.

THE FORSYTH AND HUNT HOMES, C. 1900. Conant Street, unpaved, runs between the houses.

THE ORIGINAL CENTER STAIRWAY. The house stood empty for several years before it was purchased by Henry J. Puhl in 1871. By the late 1800s, Peter M. Puhl was practicing the innovative art of portrait photography in a downstairs studio. The bay window on the east facade was added to provide him extra light. The house remained in the Puhl family until 1978. Mayo and Joan Roe acquired the home in 1988. After four years of restoration, taking care to preserve significant interior features such as the stairway with delicately turned balusters, walnut woodwork, and original hardware, the Roes moved into the house in 1992.

THE ROBERT FORSYTH HOUSE (BUILT c.1826) AT 116 EAST HARRISON, 2002. (NRHP) The clean rectangular lines with gabled roof, plain frieze running the length, and matching end chimneys are typical of the Federal era. The classical central entranceway flanked by sidelights and symmetrically placed windows reflect both Federal and Greek revival influences. The finely detailed entrance porch with double columns supporting a stylized frieze and triangular pediment with ornamental triglyph on the front facade may be a later Greek revival addition. A broad porch across the rear overhangs the lower floor which once housed the kitchen and Forsyth's office. Here he could oversee activity at the steamboat landing below. Several horses were quartered in a large barn at the rear of the property. Forsyth, in addition to his mercantile activities, was appointed Indian Agent shortly after his arrival and was responsible for distributing Indian annuities and providing government services to the Ottawa, including overseeing their safe removal. Thus, legend relates that visiting Ottawa were often fed and sheltered by Forsyth and his wife, Almira Hull. Forsyth received several grants from the Ottawa and made much of his fortune in land speculation. At his death in 1864, he was praised as a man of "eminent integrity and intelligence."

THE JOHN HUNT HOUSE (BUILT C. 1827) AT 102 WEST HARRISON, C. 1900. Tradition relates that when Robert Forsyth constructed his new home, Mary Hunt wanted an identical one near her friend and fellow member of the Methodist Meeting Circle, Almira Forsyth. Hunt complied, and the two families became neighbors as well as business partners until they severed their mercantile relationship. Forsyth became an ardent Whig and supporter of William Henry Harrison for president. Hunt remained a staunch Democrat and campaigned for the nomination of his wife's brother-in-law, Lewis Cass. Hunt followed Forsyth as mayor of Maumee in 1840 and was elected to the state legislator in 1839 and 1841. He served as a member of the state constitutional convention in 1850–51, and was elected treasurer of Lucas County from 1851–53 when he received appointment as postmaster and moved to Toledo where he died in 1877. The Hunt house has undergone several remodeling efforts, the most radical in the 1930s when the original ridge roof line with matching chimneys was transformed into a California Bungalow.

THE HUNT HOUSE, C. 1980

THE KNAGGS HOUSE, 2001.

THE GEORGE KNAGGS HOUSE (BUILT C. 1828) AT 2323 RIVER ROAD, C. 1930. The Knaggs House, built on an early Ottawa Indian grant to Whitmore Knaggs of several thousand acres of riverfront land, is among the earliest homes in the Maumee Valley. Whitmore, son of a Detroit Indian agent, trader, and former English officer, was born near Ft. Miami in 1763 and served as a scout and interpreter for the American forces during the War of 1812. His son, George, a successful business man and civic leader, built this home for his bride, Matilda Lee, shortly after their marriage in 1828. Matilda's eastern background and cultivated tastes are reflected in the details of the Federal-style house, including the wide front entranceway surrounded by sidelights, fanlight and detailed walnut woodwork, as well as the elegant interior furnishings. Supported by walnut and oak beams, the Knaggs House has undergone several "modernizations," including the wide, sweeping veranda, but still retains its initial charm.

After Matilda's death in 1847, George married Laura Bosley of Perrysburg. Their only child, Marie Antoinette, educated at Ursuline College, was considered eccentric by her peers, but had strong business instincts and was the first woman elected to the Maumee Board of Education. She was an advocate of the Interurban but is said to have "hitched" rides into Toledo, rather than pay the fare. George died in 1866 and Laura (later Mrs. Chauncey Keyser) in 1916. Unable to maintain the large estate, Antoinette sold the land to Lucas County in 1929 for the Lucas County Children's Home and moved the house across the street. The house later became a convalescence home until purchased by John Steinman, the current owner.

THE JAMES KNAGGS HOUSE (BUILT c. 1830S) AT 1308 RIVER ROAD, c. 1930S. A short distance downriver is the home of George's brother James Knaggs and his wife Therese (Campau), also located on the Knaggs grant. James, George and John had earlier continued their father's trading operation and established a post near Fort Miami. In 1825, Whitmore gave his three sons adjacent tracts of land fronting on the Maumee River where each built a home. John's home was said to have been located west of James' home. The wedding of John and Malinda Gunn in 1823 was the social event of the season, uniting two pioneer families. James was active in the commercial activities of the area and accrued considerable property as a result of his dealings with the Ottawa Indians. His handsome Greek revival home is defined by the classic doorway with sidelights and transom framed by reeded pilasters, and a wide cornice. (Courtesy of T/LCL.)

THE JAMES KNAGGS HOUSE, 2001.

THE WOLCOTT HOUSE, 2000.

THE JAMES WOLCOTT HOUSE (BUILT C. 1830) AT 1031 RIVER ROAD, C. 1910. (NRHP) This Federal-style home overlooking the Maumee River began as a one-and-half-story log cabin, built by James Wolcott, a Connecticut emigrant, and Mary Wells Wolcott, the granddaughter of Chief Little Turtle. They purchased 300 acres with money received from the U.S. government for her share of former Miami Indian lands conferred at the Treaty of 1818. The house expanded over time as the family grew in size and prominence. Mary spent many years in Kentucky with the family of her father, noted Indian scout and agent, William Wells. This heritage is reflected in the two-story porticoed veranda and the slender reeded columns crafted by local artisan, R.J. Murray. Sidelights with bent wood insets surrounding the front entranceway are similar to a pattern by Asher Benjamin, as is the graceful self-supporting stairway in the central hallway, which winds to the second floor. The woodwork, fireplace surrounds, and paneling are of native walnut. James Wolcott, a successful merchant, ship builder, and land developer, was president of the first village council in 1838 and elected mayor in 1843. When Wolcott died in 1873, the house passed to his daughter, Mary Ann, and her husband, Smith Gilbert, mayor of Maumee from 1859 to 1865. Wolcott's son, James M. (Tip), continued to live here and was elected mayor in 1887 and 1888. The house remained in the family until 1957, when Wolcott's great granddaughter, Rilla Hull, willed it to be left as a museum. It was acquired by the Maumee Valley Historical Society and is the "flagship" of the Wolcott Museum Complex. Furnishings in the house reflect the period 1830–1850 and include several original pieces.

THE DR. DANIEL COOK HOUSE (BUILT *c.* 1834) AT 208 ELIZABETH, *c.* 1940s. The long sloping rear roofline is the defining characteristic of this home and is evolved from the New England custom of attaching a lean-to on the rear of the building. It is called a "saltbox" because of the likeness to early kitchen saltboxes. Both Federal and Greek Revival elements are exhibited in the windows on the front facade and the simply framed entranceway. The house was built by Daniel Cook, a Revolutionary War surgeon who brought his family from Connecticut in 1834. Later owners include Peter and Mary Pilliod from the 1920s through 1951. The Pilliod family was among the earliest residents of Maumee. Peter farmed Pilliod Island in the Maumee River for many years, transporting his team and wagon by raft. R.E. Ansted, the following owner, made some modern improvements in the interior, but the only exterior change has been an addition on the rear of the building made by a later owner, Ruston Ayers, president of the Maumee Historical Society in the 1960s.

THE COOK HOUSE, 2001.

ST. PAUL'S RECTORY AND CHURCH, 2001.

ST. PAUL'S RECTORY AND CHURCH (BUILT *C.* 1830) AT 313 EAST WAYNE, *C.* 1925. Referred to as the "farm house" by early parishioners, this house was originally located on the corner of Elizabeth and Wayne Streets when the land for the church was acquired in 1841. It served as a home for the Reverend Mark Jukes and his wife, Harriet, and their seven children. Both Mark and Harriet, after tending the sick, fell victim to the cholera epidemic that swept Maumee in 1854. John Swan and his family resided here during his ministry from 1859 to 1874, and his son, William, recalled that the house was in poor condition at that time. The Swans lived here until 1874 and daughter Agnes, remembered as the village music teacher, served as organist and choir director for over 30 years. The house was permanently acquired by the church in 1883. Preparations were underway in 1934 to move the house to the lot east of the church where the Rathbun House stood for many years. The original frame building was turned with gable end facing the church and a frame addition was added on the east. The front facade was faced with brick veneer and a central entranceway with Greek detailing was added. A number of improvements "modernized" the interior. The house continues to serve as a rectory.

THE MOORE/HEYWOOD HOUSE (BUILT C. 1830) AT 219 EAST WAYNE, C. EARLY-1900S. The architecture and oral tradition of this Federal-style home suggest that it was built prior to 1835. The simple, symmetrical facade with an unadorned cornice and gabled ends is similar to the Forsyth House. The central entranceway with classic triangular pediment and reeded pilasters may be a later addition. The house was purchased by the Lawton family in 1844 and son, Henry, a hero of the Spanish American War, spent his early childhood here. John Moore, who emigrated from Connecticut in 1836 with George Spencer and established "Spencer and Moore," specializing in "dry goods, groceries and crockery," next purchased the home. By 1845, Moore and Spencer were involved in shipbuilding and forwarding. Moore was elected mayor of Maumee in 1851. In 1854, when John moved to Toledo to become a director of the Second National Bank, he sold the home to his brother, Elias, who had followed him to Maumee and opened his own store in 1847. Grace Moore, Elias's granddaughter, related that the kitchen and cellar were added by her grandparents. (The original kitchen was at the bottom of the back stairway.) Elias closed his store in 1872 and was appointed postmaster the following year. He also served on the Maumee School Board. Elias died in 1899 and his descendants continued to live in the house until 1921. The best remembered was a niece, Miss Nell Nicks, who lived with the Moore family. A graduate of the Boston Candy School, she was known as "the cookie lady." The only exterior changes to the house are the removal of a front portico and the addition of a screened porch by present owners, Bill and Freddi Heywood. (Courtesy of T/LCL.)

THE MOORE HOUSE, 2002.

The Linnard House (Built c. 1835) at 618 Pierce Street, 2001. This early brick Greek Revival home, with hip roof and stone lintels over six-over-six windows, was known as the Fairchild homestead when purchased by Leonard Linnard in the 1950s. The house had been "modernized" in the early 20th century and the original mantelpieces replaced with art deco tiles and scrollwork, and a narrow Victorian porch stretched across the front facade. The Leonards restored the fireplaces, opened up an original kitchen fireplace, and replaced the porch with a small portico with graceful columns supporting a narrow cornice, in keeping with the original architecture. The columned breezeway and garage were carefully matched in style and texture. Jim and Julie Frank have been the owners since 1994.

Elm Cottage (Built c. 1835) at 312 West Harrison, 2001. (NRHP) This modest brick home built in the side of the hill derives its name from the famous Elm which once provided its shade. Although oral tradition places the building date at 1830, brick buildings were more common after 1835, at the same time that Greek Revival detailing was making an impact on the Maumee Valley. The slender pilasters and transom with hand blown glass in the entranceway, the six-over-six windows on the street level, and the eyebrow windows on the top floor below the tin roof are typical Greek Revival elements. It is thought that the lower floor below street level was originally used to house livestock. The wrought-iron stars on the front facade connect to rods that once supported the walls. Original fireplaces are found in several rooms. The banister on the first-floor stairway and the sunroom at the rear of the house were added in 1929 by owner Claire Hoffman. The current owner, Craig Van Horston, continues to enjoy and preserve the home's unique qualities without disturbing its architectural integrity.

Chapter 2
1835–1850

"Nothing but a Grecian Temple is now deemed a suitable residence for a man in this Classical time."

James Fenimore Cooper, 1838

Indeed, throughout America, skilled craftsmen, following the pattern books of such architects as Asher Benjamin, turned out whole villages of neat Greek Revival homes. Public buildings, too, such as Maumee's Lucas County Courthouse, inevitably reflected America's fascination with the classic forms, although the true Greek Temple was found less often in domestic architecture. The House of Four Pillars, built in the mid-1830s at the height of Maumee's speculative activity, is an outstanding example of Greek Revival architecture. On the front gable end, four massive Doric columns rise to support the triangular pediment. The pilasters at each end of the front facade, the classic doorway, and the six-over-six panes and heavy lintels are typical Greek Revival features.

HOUSE OF FOUR PILLARS (BUILT C. 1836) AT 322 EAST BROADWAY, 2000. (NRHP)

The Secret Basement Room of Four Pillars, 1941. This Greek Revival home, built by Henry K. Steele, wholesale dealer in groceries and provisions, in the 1830s, has had several notable owners during its long history. The Underground Railroad connection possibly originated with Anderson, brother of known abolitionist David Anderson. During Anderson's ownership in the early 1840s, a deep ravine led from this "secret" basement room to the Maumee River. After Anderson left in 1849 to seek his fortune in the California gold rush, General James Steedman, of Civil War fame, briefly resided here. However, the most notorious residents were Henry Wood, editor of the *Toledo Blade* and his wife, Maude, first female City Reporter. The Woods purchased the house in 1894 and their "bohemian" lifestyle kept Maumee tongues wagging. Their most famous guest was Theodore Drieser, who composed some of his novel, *Sister Carrie*, while living at Four Pillars. Drieser purchased the house in 1899, but sold it in 1902 and returned to the East.

Lawyer and civic leader, John Ormand, bought the property in 1914. Ormand played an active role in the community, organized the Maumee Improvement Association, served on the school board, and was instrumental in bringing the Carnegie Library to Maumee. His wife was active in various civic and literary groups. After Ormand's death in 1939, the house remained vacant and a target for vandals. When William Hankins purchased the property in 1941, it was inhabited by rodents and falling into general disrepair. Undeterred, Hankins, a Toledo businessman and civic leader and his wife, Margaret, began a lengthy restoration which continued after his son, Bruce, and wife, Joan, became owners in 1969. The current owners, Fred and Susan Collar, continue to be stewards of this historic property. The House of Four Pillars is an Ohio landmark and is an example of historic preservation at its best.

Rear View of the House of Four Pillars, 1941.

THE MITCHELL/RHONEHOUSE HOUSE (BUILT C. 1836) AT 219 WEST WAYNE, 2001. (NRHP) Yet another variation on the temple style is this Greek Revival home with half-pillars forming a porticoed porch beneath a wide frieze and matching pilasters on the upper story. A triangular pediment covers the front gable end. During the early 1900s, the bottom of the pillars was cut off to accommodate a stone porch. They were restored by John Allmier. The home was built by Rueben B. Mitchell, whose father, Edward, manufactured agricultural implements in his foundry (Buttergilt Building) on Wayne Street. Rueben and Daniel Cook formed Mitchell and Cook (Union Deposit Bank), the first locally-owned banking house in Maumee. In 1896, he became co-owner of the Reynolds Mills. Dr. George E. Rhonehouse purchased the house in the 1890s, added an office wing, and practiced homeopathic medicine here for 44 years. His son, William, an ear, eyes, and nose specialist, practiced here for several years until his untimely death in a car/train accident while making a house call in 1932. Dr. James Schaal and his family were residents from the mid-1930s to the 1970s. During World War II, residents signed a petition to defer him from the draft as he was one of only two physicians remaining in Maumee. The main block of the house, with original fireplaces and woodwork, was a single family home until the late 1980s and has undergone few changes.

VIEW OF EAST BROADWAY, C. 1908. The Hanson House is on the Left, Ormand House on the right.

THE HANSON HOUSE AT 405 EAST BROADWAY, *C.* 1915. (NRHP) This side view shows Mrs. Alice Hanson with her Great Dane, Cedric, and sons Melvin and Chester Hanson. (Courtesy Helen Hanson Bamford.)

THE CLAFLIN/RIGGS/HANSON HOUSE, 2001. This handsome home exhibits many Greek Revival details, including the wide cornice returning on the gable end, centered with a fanlight with delicate tracery, and the six-over-six windows topped with matching cornices extending over wide molding. Narrow pilasters extend from the entablature on each corner. Although the original builder is not known, an 1839 transaction refers to a "tenement" on the property, purchased by Daniel Williams, a Maumee postmaster, for $1,050 at a Sheriff's Sale. In 1913, the obituary of Thomas Owens Williams referred to the "Riggs" home as his family home. George Claflin, an executive with the *Toledo Blade*, purchased the home in 1868 for son, George Jr. of Maumee. (The Claflin paper mill was located on W. Broadway near the "mill race."). In 1898, Henry E. Riggs of Toledo purchased the home and two adjacent lots for $2,200 to provide his family the benefits of clean, country air. The house had seven rooms and sat on the middle lot. An old orchard occupied the east lot and the west housed a chicken yard and cow pasture. Professor Riggs remodeled the kitchen, enlarged the back parlor, put in a bathroom, enlarged the dining room, and put in a windmill. Later, he added a wing in the back and another on the west side to accommodate his growing family.

Interior of the Hanson House, c. 1915. This Christmas scene in the back living room shows off the decorative molding below the ceiling. Chester Hanson, a Toledo businessman and Maumee community leader, purchased the house from Riggs in 1915. Hanson, like Ormand, was instrumental in bringing the Carnegie Library to Maumee and was a trustee and secretary of the Library Board for many years. At the time the Hanson family arrived, most of the surrounding acreage was undeveloped and provided a natural playground for the six children and their neighbors. A favorite spot was the tennis court built by the older boys. The house remains in the family today.

The Griswold/Richards/Herbert House (Built c. 1840s) at 228 East Broadway, 2001. (NRHP) A few doors west stands a smaller but equally pleasing version of the Greek Revival style, home to the Griswold family for many years. William P. Griswold, proprietor of Griswold's Variety Store on West Wayne Street, was also a dentist and a gunsmith. Henry P. "Peck," his son and successor in the mercantile business, was the last of the family to live in the homestead. Peck was known for his unusual habit of walking backwards, a peculiarity which resulted in a freak accident in which he was struck and killed by a hit-and-run motorist in 1934, the first pedestrian fatality in Maumee. Peck had no heirs and the house passed through several hands and "modernizations" until John and Norma Richards purchased it and began restoration in 1941. During the 1950s, the back yard became the setting for Norma Richard's popular "Backyard Theater." The stewardship of this historic home continued with Dorothy Herbert from 1969 to 1998, and current owners, Mr. and Mrs. Richard Heyman.

The Waite House, 2001.

Morrison Waite House (Built c. 1830s) at 301 West Harrison, 1931. (NRHP) Slim, reeded pilasters frame the front entry and the triple paned transom of this Greek Revival home. Six-over-six paned windows are symmetrically placed across the front facade and the wide cornice runs under the roofline and returns upon the gabled ends. It was built by Samuel Young, Maumee attorney and first auditor of Lucas County, who briefly shared the house with his law partner, Morrison R. Waite, a recent Yale graduate who arrived in Maumee in 1838, and retailer, John Moore. Waite and his wife, Amelia, resided here from 1840 until 1850. Waite participated in the civic development of Maumee, served as an early police officer, member of the volunteer fire department, and contributed to the construction of the first Lucas County Courthouse. He was elected mayor of Maumee in 1846 and to the Ohio Legislature in 1849. An active Whig, he helped organize the local Republican Party. In 1871, he was appointed to the Tribunal of Arbitration to settle U.S. claims resulting from the Civil War, and in 1874 he presided over the Ohio Constitutional Convention. Waite's greatest honor came that same year when he was appointed as Chief Justice of the U.S. Supreme Court. While in Washington, Mrs. Waite was instrumental in raising funds for the Washington Monument. Francis Nichols, as associate judge of Lucas County during the county seat controversy, and a Lucas County Clerk of Court, resided here briefly. A century later, Lardner and Martha Morris restored the home, removed the porch, and uncovered the classic details. (Courtesy of Dru Hazard.)

THE RICHARDSON/DAY HOUSE (BUILT C. 1840) AT 309 EAST HARRISON, 1931. (NRHP) This house is an excellent example of a less pretentious adaptation of the Greek Revival style. The off-center doorway located in the gable is surrounded by simple pilasters and entablature. A wide cornice returns briefly on the front facade. An early owner was Mark Richardson, a Methodist minister, entrepreneur, civic leader, and owner of the tannery located below the mill race that ran nearby. Richardson emigrated from Ireland and settled in Maumee in 1849. He lived here with his wife and seven children for the remainder of his life. His two maiden daughters, Miss Ella and Miss Emma, were content to live out their lives caring for their family home and leading the fight to preserve the ancient Elm. Ralph and Harriet Day purchased the house in 1944, removed the Victorian porch and restored the home, retaining its simple classic lines. Current owners Dan and Claudia Stein continue to preserve the home's integrity. (Courtesy of Dru Hazard.)

THE RICHARDSON/DAY HOUSE, 2001.

The Stout/Utterback House, 2001.

Stout/Utterback House (Built c. 1837) at 316 West Harrison, 1960s. (NRHP) Dr. William St. Clair, who briefly operated the Eagle Tavern, is the original owner of this property overlooking the river and the projected canal route. At that time, most of the commerce was on the flats and on Front Street (now a paper street below Harrison). This house exhibits Federal and early-Classical influences. Six-over-six windows are placed symmetrically across the front facade under a simple uncluttered roofline. The arched entranceway with a fanlight extending over sidelights framed by slender columns is a carry-over from the Federal period. Decorators Claire and Geraldo Pheatt Hoffman owned the home in the 1930s and converted it into a duplex. Dr. S.B. Stout, who practiced dentistry in Maumee for many years, purchased the home from the Hoffman's. Sue and Robert Utterback, the current owners, returned the house to a single family home and restored many period features such as the handsome entranceway.

THE WILKINSON/VAN FLEET HOUSE (BUILT *C.* 1836) AT 233 WEST HARRISON, *C.* 1900. (NRHP) The square pillars supporting a narrow cornice under the porch roof are unusual stylistic variations of Greek Revival. A wider entablature runs under the gabled roof and returns over an arched window with wooden fanlight and palladium style window. The off-center doorway leads into the entrance hall with a handsome staircase. The small enclosed porch, once recessed and columned, led into a summer kitchen. Woodwork throughout the house is typical of the period. The unusual disproportion between the lower floor and upper floors gave rise to the legend that the house was built to resemble a "steamboat." Indeed, the builder, James Wilkinson, was a member of a family of ship captains and was a ship builder. He served as mayor of Maumee from 1841 to 1843. The family suffered a great tragedy in 1849 when the steamer piloted by his step-son, Charles C. Roby, exploded and sank on Lake Erie. Wilkinson's wife, Alice, granddaughter, Abby Champion, Captain Roby and his wife, Alice, were all drowned. More fortunate was a later owner, Colonel Henry Van Fleet, who was captured at Chickamauga and imprisoned at Andersonville during the Civil War. He was among a shipload of freed prisoners when their craft, the *Sultana*, caught fire and sank. Van Fleet was one of the few to survive. Van Fleet later served several terms on Maumee City Council and was elected county commissioner in 1906. Previously, the Lautzenheiser family who operated the Maumee Woolen Mill from *c.*1875 to the early-1900s lived here. Tom and Molly Ehni purchased the home from Hugh and Bunny Price in the 1980s and have preserved the home's classic architecture.

THE VAN FLEET HOUSE, 2001.

THE ST. CLAIR/DIDIER HOUSE, 2001.

THE ST. CLAIR/DIDIER HOUSE (BUILT *c.* 1845) AT 205 WEST BROADWAY, 1930. (NRHP) The brick home of William St. Clair presents a different interpretation of Greek Revival. The older portion of the house may have been built in the mid-1830s, when brick became available. The window lintels are frame and the original doorway leads into the kitchen (once a large living area) with a wood burning fireplace. The architecture of the front block is in keeping with the mid-1840s. A wide cornice runs under the hip roof and around the front portico, supported by fluted pillars. Two-story Doric columns support the cornice of a recessed side porch where the two sections connect. Dr. St. Clair, a Harvard graduate, emigrated from Maine in 1837. His first wife, Laura, died soon after arrival. St. Clair and his second wife, Eliza, probably lived here until 1858, when he sold the home and moved west. The property was in financial litigation and occupied by renters during the Civil War years. Patrick and Celia Dowling owned the home from 1885 to 1925 and their son, Michael, operated a lunchroom or tavern here for several years. During the 1930s, Page and Esther Lindsay operated a tea room. In 1971, after several changes in ownership, Charles and Mary Didier returned the house to a family home and restored many of the original details. Interior features include an elegant, curving staircase and a front parlor with heavy woodwork and cornices above the high windows.

GIBBS HOUSE (BUILT C. 1838) AT 209 WEST HARRISON, C. 1900. (NRHP) One of the finest examples of Greek Revival architecture is this two-story home. Reeded pilasters at each corner and on either side of the entranceway give the appearance of columns, a common variation of Greek Revival Temple style. The symmetrical placement of six-over-six windows and classical doorway with sidelights and transom are also typical. The most unique feature is the dentil cornice which runs underneath the roofline and returns on the gable ends. The house is thought to have been completed by Chloe Spafford Gilbert Gibbs, of the pioneer Spafford family and widow of Almon Gibbs, a quartermaster at Fort Meigs in 1814, who, in partnership with Horatio Conant, operated a retail business below East Harrison Street and was prominent among the early founders of Maumee. George Utter, a Civil War veteran who resided here in the 1890s, is pictured with his wife in this early photo. William Tecumseh O'Hara, a colorful Lucas County prosecutor, lived here in the 1930s. In the mid-60s, owners Lee and Sue Slayton began the laborious job of removing the stucco from the front facade. Their restoration efforts were continued by successive owners; Jeff and Barbara Day are currently stewards of this historic property.

THE GIBBS HOUSE, 2001.

William Dix (Dicks) House (Built 1841–1847) at 422 W. Broadway, 1930s. (NRHP) This house probably began as a simple Greek Revival home but somewhere in the several years it took to complete, it acquired some elements of the Italianate style, just making its appearance in the United States. The basic floor plan and the symmetrical front facade and gabled roof are typical Greek Revival. The bracketed consoles under the roofline instead of the customary cornice, the decorative ironwork in a magnolia pattern (also a popular ante-bellum trend), and the carved stone lintels are hallmarks of the Italianate style. The interior reflects the Greek Revival period both in floor plan and elaborate detailing of the woodwork. The house is supported with hewn walnut timbers and retains its original wood paneling throughout. A finely detailed "Adamesque" mantelpiece was installed by a later owner. A winding mahogany staircase leads to the second floor. William Dix moved to Maumee from Mississippi and entered into a partnership with his friend, George Reynolds, also of Mississippi, who was "disgusted with the results of slavery" and preferred to live in a "free state," to build and operate the Pearl (flour) Mill. In 1859, Reynolds sold out to Dix. Meanwhile, Dix served on village council and took an active part in the community. After his death in 1879, his descendants continued to live in the family home. The last residents were his granddaughters, Lucille and Gladys Bachelder (Stanley) and "Aunt Phoebe," the resident ghost whose presence has been felt by subsequent owners.

The Dix House, 2001. Harold and Wanda Meyers purchased the home in 1948 and began its restoration, including removal of the heavy ivy growth which covered its fine stylistic features. Current owners, William and Linda Fayerweather, continue preservation of both the house and its attractive gardens.

OSCAR WHITE HOME (BUILT *C.* 1840S) AT 411 WEST BROADWAY, 2002. (NRHP) A bay window, a broad veranda with bracketed roof and double door entrance added over the years give this Greek Revival home a Victorian appearance. The interior remains classical in floor plan and stylistic details. An elegant curving staircase in the front entranceway leads to the second floor and woodwork and window treatments throughout are of the Greek Revival period. The home was built by Dr. Oscar White, a recent graduate of Dartmouth College, who arrived in Maumee in 1827 and entered a partnership with Dr. Horatio Conant. They were the only fully accredited physicians at the time. Their practice extended up the Maumee River to Defiance, and included Adrian, Blissfield, and Monroe, Michigan. White married Maria Jackson, daughter of James Jackson, Government Indian Agent at Maumee, and in 1831was commissioned to vaccinate the Indians in the vicinity for smallpox. White dabbled in real estate, served on the Whig central Committee, was a member of the Maumee Merchants Association, and served on the Lucas County Board of Health. Longtime residents include the Clarence M. Bloomer family, which resided here from the late-1800s through the mid-1900s. A portrait of their daughter, Carrie Bloomer, still has a place of honor in the house. Some residents believe that they still hear the rustle of her skirts on the stairway. Current owners, the Steven Sokolskys, continue to maintain the architectural integrity of the historic home.

CARRIE BLOOMER. She continues to observe the activities of successive owners from her portrait inside the entrance hall, *c.* early-1900s.

THE THOMPSON BUILDING, 2002.

MOVING THE FRANCES E. THOMPSON HOUSE (BUILT C. 1840S) TO 123 WEST DUDLEY, 1953. Cornices and pilasters capped with reeded blocks and dentil trim surround the lower windows of this Greek Revival building. A palladium-style window is centered in the gable end and the front entranceway is reached through a pedimented portico. A second doorway is surrounded by sidelights. From the late-19th to the mid-20th century, Francis Thompson operated his flower shop from his home at 216 Conant Street and was known for the beautiful calla lilies that he grew in his greenhouse, long after he retired. Thompson was active in the community and served two terms as mayor, 1832 and 1836. In 1953, Lester Martin purchased the old home, moved it to its new location, and converted it to offices without drastically altering the original lines of the building. It has since been converted to apartments.

The Wusterfeld /Mauer House (Built c. 1845) at 725 West Broadway, 1932. (NRHP) This brick, two-story home exemplifies all the markings of the Greek Revival style. A wide frieze runs under the gable roof which is supported by hand-hewn beams and the six-over-six windows are crowned with stone lintels. Henry Forsyth owned the property in 1845 and a sharp rise in taxes suggests that the house was built at that time. Dr. Ernst Wusterfeld purchased the home in 1863 and it remained in his family until the 1970s. Physicians in small communities, lacking hospital facilities, often kept patients in their own homes for observation, treatment, and isolation. What formerly served as an office is now a den where shelves that held medical supplies display books and collectibles. The property was left to daughter, Wilhimina, who lived here for several years after the Doctor's death in 1883. "Minna" and her brother, William, divided and sold the remainder in 1890. After Minna's death in 1922, the house, referred to by neighbors as "Toad Hall," was overgrown and in serious disrepair until purchased by Buck and Wimsey Dillon in 1970. During several years of major restoration, the Dillons enlarged several small rooms and added a family room and a greenhouse. Current owners, Terry and Judy Mauer, continue to preserve this historic home.

The Mauer House, 2001.

THE SERVAIS HOUSE, 2001.

BOTTORFF/SERVAIS HOUSE (BUILT 1845–1850) AT 504 W. BROADWAY, 1960. The Greek Revival details on this home were obscured by later additions and siding until the current owners uncovered the wide frieze board under the gabled roof. The handsome classic doorway is flanked with turned double pillars, sidelights, and glass transom. Contrasting colors of paint emphasize the six-over-six windows and moldings. A small addition, once a separate apartment, has been incorporated into the one-family home. This was the home of the Fernand Bottorff family from 1930s, until purchased by the current owners, Mr. and Mrs. Steve Servais.

OLD METHODIST PARSONAGE (BUILT *C.* 1840S) AT 128 WEST BROADWAY, *C.* 1915. Greek Revival influence can be seen in the classic entranceway with cornice and pilasters surrounding the door and in windows on the front façade. A small bay was added during the early 1920s. The house was built on West Broadway, which remained unpaved until 1916, next to the Methodist Church. It was moved to 201 West Dudley Street in the 1960s, when St. Joseph Catholic Church purchased the property for expansion of their school and community center. The last Methodist minister to live at the Broadway address was the Reverend W.L. Stafford.

201 WEST DUDLEY, 2001.

The Miller Home, 2001.

John Miller House (Built c. 1840s) at 721 Pierce, c. 1890s. The most outstanding feature of this early Greek Revival house is the front entranceway, with door and sidelights surrounded by a heavy entablature over matching pilasters. An early photo shows a narrow cornice under the roofline and six-over-six windows in the otherwise simple facade. The house was built by John Miller, who, with his wife Barbara, emigrated from Bavaria. A unique feature of the house is a mural of Prussian soldiers painted by John, which is still visible today. Flags on both the Republican and the Democratic flagpoles at Miami flew at half mast during the political campaign of 1884, when Mr. Miller was killed in a highly publicized streetcar accident while he was leading the Democratic procession down Tenth Street in Toledo. John's grandson, Fred Miller, a road-master on the Toledo, Bowling Green, & Southern Railroad, was the last of three generations to live in the family home. The current residents are preserving the home's historical and architectural integrity.

The Frederick House/Talking Turtle Shop (Built c. 1842*) at 1031 River Rd, 1966 on Original Site. This typical Greek Revival townhouse was originally located at 133 East Wayne Street at the site of the municipal parking lot. It was moved by owner Charles Reynolds and donated to the Maumee Valley Historical Society in 1971. Although additions have been made over the years, the original features, including the wide cornice returning on the gable end, the six-over-six windows, and the symmetrical front facade with narrow pilasters at each corner are indicative of the period. "Eyebrow" windows are cut into the cornice of the east facade. The home had two wings at one time. The east wing was removed in 1918 to add a sunroom. The house was known as the Frederick Homestead for many years. J.K. Fredericks was proprietor of a grocery store in Maumee from 1864 to 1892 when his son, M. "Percy," took over. Percy retired in 1939 and he and his wife, Alice (Rodd), continued to occupy the home until their deaths in the mid-1960s. Since removal to the grounds of the Lucas County/Maumee Valley Historical Society, the Victorian front porch was removed and the exterior restored to its original charm. The Society has been careful to keep the interior faithful to the period. (*Date given by M.P. Fredericks in 1938.)

The Frederick House, 2001.

The Spangler/Gosline House (Built *c.* 1837) at 232 East Wayne, 2001. (NRHP) This two-story frame home with a pedimented front gable and semicircular fanlight is an excellent example of modified Greek Revival, emphasized by the front entranceway with pilasters and frieze, although the usual heavy entablature is lacking. A small Victorian side porch is trimmed with scrollwork. The earliest known owner was Elizabeth Rundel, who purchased the house in 1875. After several successive owners, the home was purchased in 1929 by Ernest Spangler of the Spangler Candy Company, famous for their "Dum Dum" lollipops. The Spanglers made many improvements, including an addition. The home was acquired by Robert Gosline, a prominent Toledo attorney and member of Maumee City Council, in the 1950s. He and his wife, Martha, made many philanthropic and civic contributions to the community while making their family home until 1999.

The Henry Reed Jr. House (Built *c.* 1840s) on White Street, 2001. (NRHP) Just a few blocks from the Spangler House is this downsized version of a Greek Revival townhouse with the characteristic wide entablature returning on the gable end. A neat classic entranceway, two matching six-over-six windows on the front façade, one centered in the half-story above, and two eyebrow windows cut into the entablature are typical features. This home was built by Henry Reed Jr., who emigrated from Connecticut in 1837. Reed quickly became an ardent booster and champion of civic improvements for Maumee. He was elected first village recorder and was active in the Whig party. Following the death of his four-year-old daughter, Amanda, in 1838, and shortly thereafter his wife, Elizabeth, Reed left Maumee for the California gold fields.

The Isaac Hull House (Built *c.* 1836) at 114 E. Harrison, 2001. (NRHP) This house retains its Greek Revival appearance with a wide frieze board returning on the gable end and asymmetrical openings in the front façade. The structure is supported by four black walnut beams bolted with iron rods, and brick walls are hidden behind the stucco. The Hull family lived on the upper floor and Hull operated a mercantile establishment on the lower level. At one time, a double door opened toward the river side. Isaac was a nephew of Commodore Hull, who commanded the *U.S.S. Constitution* during the War of 1812. An Uncle, William, was the commander at Fort Detroit, when it surrendered to the British. His brother, David, was among the first settlers prior to 1812. After the war, the remainder of the family immigrated to the Maumee Valley. Isaac was known for his feats of physical endurance and it was said that he often walked between Maumee and Defiance, Ohio, in a single day to look after his various business interests. Isaac and his wife, Chloe (Spafford), built this home near his sister, Almira, and her husband, Robert Forsyth.

The Creps/Tallman House (Built *c.* 1840s) at 526 W. Broadway, 2001. A wide frieze extending completely under the roofline, the classic off-center doorway with side lights, and the six-over-six windows are all typical elements of modest Greek Revival townhouses found throughout Maumee. The interior also follows the classic pattern with solid walnut beams in the construction, a pine stairway with walnut banister, and walnut paneling. Among the early owners were Abner Backus, an area grain dealer and the first canal collector; and Rosanna Creps, who purchased the home in 1864. Archie Creps, a local building contractor, was an active member of the Masonic Lodge. Local tradition relates that the front door was originally part of the old Masonic Hall. John and Cynthia Galbraith purchased the home in 1946 from Archie Creps' estate and installed indoor plumbing and modern electrical wiring and heating. The current owners are the John Tallman family who have added their own touches to the house and the gardens.

THE AMASA WINSLOW HOUSE (BUILT *c.* 1838) AT 315 CASS STREET, 2001. (NRHP) This small cottage is a rare example of a brick Greek revival saltbox with stone lintels and a shallow roof, sometimes referred to as a "cat slide," sloping to the rear. A narrow cornice runs under the roof with a slight return on the end. Three iron plates on each gable end connect with a supporting rod. The builder was Amasa Winslow, an early blacksmith who owned and operated a foundry in the adjacent building, known later as the Pauken Broom Factory. Winslow, a New Englander, held strong anti-slavery sentiments and is said to have occasionally hidden a runaway in his barn. During the 1930s, this was the family home of Dennis Gay, a well-loved custodian of Union School.

THE RICHARDSON/WINZELER HOUSE ((BUILT *c.* 1837) AT 215 WEST HARRISON, 2001. (NRHP) This modest, unadorned cottage is noted for being the home of Mrs. Alta Winzeler Richardson, beloved Maumee schoolteacher/storyteller and custodian of local lore. Alta's parents purchased the one-and-a-half-story house in 1907 and she later inherited the property. Alta later recalled that there were no houses across the street and only the Wilkinson and Gibbs houses on the north side of the block. Her grandfather, Jacob Winzeler, a stone mason from Switzerland, carved the stone lintels on Union School when it was built in 1870; and when the third floor was removed, Alta saved some of the stones for a front step. Alta filled her house with memorabilia of Maumee and its residents and was always willing to share their story with visitors.

Chapter 3

1850–1865

"[Maumee] is a very pretty town [although] a very straggling town with here and there the forest trees still standing."

Harriet Jukes, letters from Maumee, 1854

The ancient trees were disappearing quickly by mid-century as sawmills were built along the "mill race" (Ford Street) between the canal and the river. George Reynolds was among the first to build a saw mill, followed by a flour mill (Pearl Mill). He soon faced competition from other entrepreneurs. By the end of the 1850s, two brick factories and a planting mill also supplied lumber and building materials to a half-dozen brick and stone masons and an equal number of carpenter/builders. Meanwhile, by 1855, the Wabash and Erie was making regular stops in Maumee, dropping off new "settlers" and supplies and escalating the need for housing.

THE CHURCH HOUSE (BUILT *C*. 1850) AT 332 WEST WAYNE STREET, 2001. Framed cornices over the windows and carved and bracketed posts on the wrap-around porch are typical Victorian embellishments on this simple frame double-gabled home. During the late 19th and into the mid-20th century, this was the home of the Church family. After George Church passed away in 1933, his daughter Lulu occupied the home until her death in 1945. Lulu was one of the "pioneer" operators at the AT&T test station. The telephone company provided one of the first "career" opportunities for women at a time when the woman's place was considered to be in the home. Lulu began as a "messenger girl" for $15 a month and worked her way up to operator, a position previously held by men. Lulu, later referred to as a "trail blazer' by Ohio Bell, worked for the company for thirty years, beginning in 1901.

THE HELTABRAKE/HELVEY HOUSE (BUILT c. 1850) AT 401 W. BROADWAY, 1960S. This home with its rectangular lines has the earmarks of the 1850s, when Greek Revival was becoming passé. With the advances in construction methods, builders and carpenters were free to adapt vernacular styles and indigenous materials to traditional patterns. The homes of the 1850s and early-1860s were more "upright," with steeper gables, and often had wings on one or both sides. Chimneys became smaller and one central chimney often sufficed to accommodate heating with stoves. This house retains the classic front facade with off-center doorway and floor plan. Early occupants include the Renslaar sisters who were tutors to the Bachelor girls, granddaughters of William Dix, in the early 1900s. Current owners, Christine and Don Helvey, carefully chose soft shades of gray highlighted with magenta, popular colors for homes of the 1850s, to accentuate the architectural features of this charming home. Period landscaping and gardens provide additional enhancements.

THE HELTABRAKE/HELVEY HOUSE, 2001.

THE L.M. MURPHY HOUSE (BUILT *c.* 1850S) AT 301 WEST BROADWAY, *c.* 1900. (NRHP) A reluctance to part with traditional patterns while embracing the latest in architectural trends is exemplified in this home. A central entranceway with sidelights and transom are typical of classic designs and an early photograph shows the original six-over-six windows with narrow lentils. Iron cresting running along the roof line and a corbelled chimney add a Gothic touch. The matching bay windows topped with brackets and cresting on flat roofs complete the Victorian effect. The house is supported by bark-covered timbers fastened with wooden pegs. Original features include shutters throughout, wide moldings, and front and back stairways. Early residents were William Burge and his wife, who celebrated their Silver Anniversary at a reception in their home in 1885, before becoming superintendent and matron of the Children's Home in 1890, respectively. The house was purchased by the L.M. Murphy family in 1891. Murphy, a noted criminal lawyer with offices in Toledo, served as Maumee Solicitor, and was known for his colorful oratory. After Murphy's death in 1929, his daughters, Maude and Edith, graduates of Hillsdale College, remained at home while teaching school and caring for their invalid mother. Maude died in 1951 and Edith continued to live in the homestead and care for brother, Bob. During her residency the Gothic trim was removed and the rear wing was added. The barn and the gazebo are original to the property.

THE L.M. MURPHY HOUSE, 2002.

309 EAST DUDLEY (BUILT *C.* 1850) 1960s. Although the construction date for this house is listed as 1862, the classical doorway with pilasters and entablature, symmetrical placement of six-over-six windows, and narrow pilasters at each corner which connect to a narrow cornice are similar to many locally built homes of the 1850s. The lower photo illustrates how these attractive features have been emphasized by the current owners.

309 EAST DUDLEY, 2001.

(Below) **THE PERRIN/GANNON/ DIBLING HOME (BUILT *C.* 1849) AT 318 EAST DUDLEY, 2001.** The wide cornice returning on the gable end and the six-over-six widows on the main block are typical of the Greek Revival townhouses found throughout Maumee. David Perrin, a ship carpenter and builder who came to Maumee in 1836, purchased the property in 1848 and completed construction probably by 1849. During the Perrin family's residency, four sons served in the Civil War and two, James and Benjamin, lost their lives. Son, David H., a builder, his wife, Mary, and three sons occupied the family home after Perrin's death in 1869. He sold this and an adjoining lot for $1,750 in 1876. The property was inherited by Clarissa Cook Moor in 1904 and ultimately was purchased by Kevin Gannon Sr. During the many years that this was the Gannon family home, a number of renovations, including a rear addition and a front porch, were added. The home is currently owned by Maumee businessman and former member of Maumee City Council, Thomas Dibling, who has restored many of the home's period features.

BORCK HOUSE (BUILT IN THE 1850S) 2222 RIVER ROAD, 1890S. This typical rectangular farmhouse is located off River Road on land which once comprised the large Henry Borck farm between Askin and Hollister. Mary Borck was one of the first employees of the Children's Home when it opened in 1890. The farmhouse remained in the Borck family until the mid-1930s, when it became the home of William McEwen, an attorney and solicitor for Maumee until 1940. The original block of the farmhouse has remained remarkably unchanged except for an addition of a veranda in the 1890s, since removed, and the rounded hood molding over the entranceway. Additions have been made to the rear of the building without altering the character of the house.

THE BORCK/MCEWEN HOUSE, 2002.

THE VAN RENSSLAER HOUSE (BUILT *C.* 1850) AT 301 WEST WAYNE, 2002. A wide cornice returning on the gable end, centered by a small fanlight, indicate that this may have been the original front facade with a doorway possibly centered between the two windows. Additions have been made on the front and rear of this transitional house. It was the home of John Van Rensslaer, a lake captain for many years until he retired in 1879 to become a grocer for the next 20 years. Oral tradition relates that he once operated a small grocery and hardware store in his home. Captain Van Rensslaer, a descendent of the Van Rensslaer patroons of New York, acquired considerable real estate and was active in community affairs. His wife, Eliza (Marston), owned the property where Fort Miami is located and served as president of the early Advisory Board of Lucas County Children's Home.

THE VAN RENSSLAER GROCERY (BUILT *C.* 1850) AT 317 WEST WAYNE, 2001. This two-story brick building is typical of many 19th century commercial structures. Heavy stone lintels and cornices frame the upper windows over the recessed windows and main entranceway on the front facade. Early owner, Sanders Van Rensslaer, took over his father's grocery business in 1892 and advertised a "full line of groceries" and "a line of Dry Goods and Notions." Sanders lived above the store until he built the house next door, as was common in the 19th and early 20th century, when people walked to work or to shop and grocery stores were located in almost every neighborhood rather than clustered in a central area. This home is now a duplex, but the facade has remained remarkably unchanged.

ETTER'S GROCERY AT THE JOHNSON/ETTER BUILDING (BUILT *C.* 1860S) AT 330 WEST WAYNE STREET, 2001. With the exception of a small elliptical window in the front facade and slightly arched upper lintels, this brick commercial building is a simple unadorned block. In 1868, Samuel Johnson willed his store and building, then occupied by William Dix, to his brother, Wakeman. Samuel and Dix were both involved in milling, and oral tradition relates that this once was a flour mill situated on the mill race, which flowed down Kingsbury to Broadway and the river. The building is best remembered as Etter's Grocery in the early 20th century. Jewell Etter operated a grocery on the first level and lived above. A separate building was added in the 1930s. The building is now a duplex.

THE POMEROY HOME (BUILT IN THE 1850S) AT 302 WEST HARRISON STREET, 1931. This home, like many built in the 1850s, follows a simple, vernacular form with few stylistic details, other than the Victorian brackets on the front porch columns (since removed). The house, overlooking the Maumee River, was for many years the home of Harry M. Pomeroy, publisher and editor of the *Advance Era* from 1910 until 1939, and postmaster from 1912 to 1920. Pomeroy moved from Toledo to Maumee in 1913 and never hesitated to boast of the merits of his adopted town, and in particular, of the "Majestic" Maumee River. He often wrote of the joys of "gazing out of [my] mansion window upon the broad expanse of the [Maumee] River." The view remains one of the home's greatest assets, although the house has expanded considerably since Pomeroy's residency. Several years after Pomeroy's death in 1952, the house was purchased by Albert and Dorothy Cassidy. The current residents, the Cassidy's granddaughter and her husband, have installed dormers to open the upstairs and are adding more living space to the side and rear of the house.

THE POMEROY/ CASSIDY HOME, 2002. The original pump remains by front porch.

The Gunn House (Built 1855–1860) at 220 West Broadway, 1960s. (NRHP) This transitional home exhibits elements of several architectural styles. The pillared portico on the west side and the interior floor plan follow the design of the Greek Revival period. However, the longer, narrow windows with heavy ornate cornices and the brackets under the roof are Gothic/ Victorian features. A pedimented portico, which was probably a later addition, was removed by the current owners. The Gunn family was among the early residents. "Grandma Gunn," as she was affectionately remembered, raised cows in the lot next door and sold her dairy products to neighbors. During the early 1900s, the Frank Gulick family, active members of the community, resided here. Daughter, Frances, was chosen "Miss Maumee" for the Maumee Historical Pageant in 1926. Son, Merle, a football star in high school, became Maumee's first All-American in 1928, while at Hobart College. He later married "the girl next door," Edna Zellar, and became a successful insurance executive in New York. In the 1960s, this was the home of Maumee mayor and councilman, Josiah Herbert and his wife, Dorothy, who was the first woman to serve on Maumee City Council.

The Gunn/Gulick House, 2001.

ST. JOSEPH SCHOOL (BUILT C. 1855) AT 415 AND 419 WEST JOHN STREET, 1880. These two frame houses, side by side on West John, were moved from St. Joseph Parish property in 1913 or 1914, when construction was begun on a new brick school. The former schoolhouse, re-located at 419, replaced the original building at the rear of the church in 1866. The simple vernacular style closely resembles the early structures, although the entrance on 419 is changed and windows have been replaced on the front facade to accommodate addition of a large chimney. Both houses have been enlarged. The house on the right may have been the Rectory.

ST. JOSEPH SCHOOL, 2001.

LUDLOW BUILDINGS, 2001.

LUDLOW BUILDING AND HOUSE (BUILT C. 1860) AT 2203 AND 2206 RIVER ROAD, C. 1900. This two-story, brick building is an excellent example of early-Victorian commercial architecture. Italianate influences are seen in the round headed windows and brick moldings above, and the bracketed roofline. The elliptical divided window panes, which are repeated in the small fanlight of the adjacent house, and the handsome doorway, are classical in feeling. The frame house follows simpler, more classical lines, with a balanced front facade and a Victorian front porch with turned posts and balustrades. Both buildings were built by the Ludlow family who operated a grocery on the lower floor and used the upper for dances and similar events. The house was occupied by the Ludlows for many years, but at one time was known as the Miami Hotel, when they took in boarders. In the 1930s, the upper floor of 2203 was converted to an apartment. Over the years, both buildings have housed a variety of uses, from apartments to mercantile establishments.

LEO ZELLER HOUSE (BUILT C. 1857) AT 409 EAST WAYNE STREET, 1957. This two-story, brick home is similar to plans for Italianate cottages by such popular architects as A.J. Bicknell and represents a departure from the simpler lines of the Greek Revival period. The arched window heads over double hung windows and doorways give an Italianate look to the otherwise vernacular block. Decorative cresting under the roofline and small porticoes at each entranceway may have once contributed to the effect. The large porch seen in the lower photo was probably added in the early-20th century. This was the home of Leo Zeller, member of a large family, including brothers Charles and William, whose parents had emigrated from Germany. The house remained in the family until the death of 93-year-old Elva Zeller, a niece, in 1999. Miss Zeller, a graduate of Maumee High School in 1916 and Bowling Green State Normal College, was a teacher in Toledo and Lucas County schools for over 40 years.

THE ZELLER HOUSE, 2001.

THE WUNDERLIN/BURDO HOUSE, 2001.

THE WUNDERLIN/BURDO HOUSE (BUILT IN THE 1860S) AT 426 EAST INDIANA AVENUE, 1951. Originally located in the 300 block of West Wayne across from St. Paul's Episcopal Church, this upright and wing house is typical of many houses of the period. It was home to the Wunderlin family for many years. It was moved in 1951, when the lots were sold for new construction. The home was purchased and moved for newlyweds, Fred and Sue Burdo, and they immediately began a lengthy restoration. The Burdos continue to maintain their historic home and although they made several additions to accommodate their growing family, including a second story on the west wing, the front facade of the original block has not been significantly altered. (Courtesy of Fred and Sue Burdo.)

THE BALLOFF/ BURDO HOUSE (BUILT c. 1850) AT 701 ELIZABETH STREET, c. 1920s. When Henry Balloff and his wife, Clarissa Lavina Burdo (Bordeaux), built their family home, they were surrounded by farmland and pasture As late as the 1920s, outbuildings were still standing and only a plank sidewalk running alongside the house indicated that the property was now within the village limits. The house is typical of the rectangular farmhouses found throughout Northwest Ohio, with a wrap-around porch and bay on the west side probably added later. The land was originally owned by Clarissa's father, Peter Bordeaux, a French-Canadian emigrant who acquired a large tract of land (including site of present day Golden Gate Shopping Center) in 1836, and much of it remained in the Balloff and Burdo families. The current owner, Helen Burdo Womack, is the great-great-granddaughter of Peter, and the niece of Margaret Balloff, who lived here for many years. The Burdo family was involved in many community organizations and activities. Peter's great grandson, Ralph Burdo, served on the Maumee Village Council for eight years, was a volunteer fireman, and was the first full-time chief of the Fire Department. The Ralph Burdo family home, which was located near Conant and Clinton Streets (site of the Pharm), was relocated to 425 East Indiana when the shopping center was built.

THE BALLOFF HOME, 2002.

THE HORATIO CONANT HOUSE (BUILT C. 1857) AT 303 WEST WILLIAMS, 2002. The home of Dr. Horatio Conant—early physician, civic leader, and merchant, and for whom Conant Street is named—moved from its original location on the corner of East Wayne Street and Conant to this site in 1956. The original entranceway is said to have faced Conant, but was turned in 1900 as that street became more commercial. Several alterations have been made, but the wide cornice under the roofline and the doorway framed by reeded pilasters and pediment enclosing a carved, fanlight design are late-Greek Revival details. A one-story bay is probably a later addition. Conant was the area's first physician and traveled all over northwest Ohio on horseback to treat the sick. He was elected mayor of Maumee in 1848.

THE WOLFINGER-GOSSENS HOUSE (BUILT C. 1856) AT 426 WEST WAYNE STREET, 2001. Although the classic doorway with sidelights and transom and the windows on the upper façade are Greek revival in style, the three-bay window classifies it as Victorian. A later addition extends from the west side. Grace Wolfinger-Gossens, a founder and first treasurer of the Woman's Relief Society in 1884, was a pioneer female insurance agent.

Daniel Cook Home, 2001. The mansard roof was the hallmark of the Second Empire style in the 1860s and 1870s. Although houses such as the Cook House may have been built at an earlier date and possess some features representative of previous periods, the addition of a Mansard roof immediately classifies it as Second Empire.

Chapter 4
1865–1900

"Each...studied the house and judged according to her own standards its architectural devices: a mansard roof, many-windowed and covered with slates in a varicolored pattern; a porte-cochere, and a side veranda..."

Observing an 1868 home in *Ladies of the Club*, by Helen Hooven Santmyer

DANIEL COOK'S SUMMER HOUSE, C. 1910.

DANIEL F. COOK HOME (BUILT 1850-1860S), AT 204 WEST DUDLEY, 1890'S. (NRHP) Although the original block of this house is earlier, the mansard roof and pure Victorian detail, added later, are the distinguishing architectural elements. A wide, bracketed cornice supports the mansard roof and large, ornate dormers penetrate the decorative shingles and allow light into the spacious third floor. A heavily ornamented and bracketed front porch and double-entry doors with etched glass panels give the house an Italianate flair. Notable interior features include the cherry staircase and early woodwork. A second stairway unites the original house with a rear addition, and a winding staircase leads to the third floor. Daniel F. Cook, son of physician Daniel Cook, arrived in Maumee in 1835, after graduation from Harvard Law School. Cook was a successful lawyer, but it was his shrewd business acumen in real estate and as a founding director of the Union Deposit Bank that brought him financial success. In 1858, Cook married Abby Frost and they began the transformation of the house into an elegant Second Empire mansion. (Courtesy of Joseph and Nancy Hendrikx.)

INTERIOR OF THE COOK HOUSE, C. 1910. Daniel Cook's nieces are sharing a book in this photo taken in the Cook parlor. Cook and his wife were active in the community and in St. Paul's Episcopal Church. Cook served several terms on the village council, was elected mayor in 1855 and 1858, and served as Lucas County Commissioner from 1854 to 1858. The Cooks had no direct descendant and thus, when Cook died in 1904, he left the house to his niece, Clarissa Moor. Miss Moor was responsible for hiring a student of Frederick Law Olmstead to landscape the grounds and plant the lilac trees and flowering shrubs that surrounded the property. She added the French doors that led to a rustic Victorian "summer house." After Clarissa's death, the house was left to Cook's great-nephew, Paul Williams, and it remained in the family until 1970. The current owners, Denny and Marcia DuBell, are committed to the preservation of the home.

INTERIOR OF THE COOK HOUSE, 2002. Bethany DuBell and friend, Eleanor Baum, enjoying a quiet moment with a book in the Cook House parlor.

THE MERRELS/ZELLER HOUSE (BUILT C. 1872) AT 231 WEST BROADWAY, 2002. (NRHP) The distinguishing feature of this two-story, brick home is its high mansard roof with iron cresting and small eyebrow windows under the bracketed cornice. Wide, carved limestone lintels and sills frame the elongated windows. A bay window extends through the third floor. Originally, the double doors with decorative glass were covered by an ornamental hood and narrow verandas with turned posts and balusters with doors to the inside flanked the east and west sides. The interior is characterized by 12-foot ceilings and wide moldings around windows extending from a heavy carved plaster cornice to wide baseboards. The house was built by Thomas Merrels, a Lucas County Commissioner who owned an agricultural implement business located in the building behind this property (Buttergilt Building). William Zeller, owner of Zellers Market on Wayne Street, purchased the home in 1909 and the family lived here until 1945. In 1915, Zeller added the wrap-around front porch, where his three daughters liked to host dancing parties. The sun porch was added by the current owners, Mr. and Mrs. Peter Wendler, in 1975.

YOUNG OLIVE ZELLER AND COUSIN, ELVA ZELLER, 1915.

THE GENNINGS HOUSE (BUILT C. 1865) AT 613 WEST BROADWAY, C. 1870. Cornices and molding around the elongated windows, and decorative brackets and posts supporting the flat roof on the matching square porches, give this double-gabled farmhouse an Italianate appearance. The brickwork on the chimney and the medallion in the front gable add to the effect. The photos illustrate the changes over the years. This was the home of Fred and Sophia Gennings family from the turn-of-the-century through the mid-1940s. Mr. Gennings was proprietor of Gennings Grocery at Ford and Wayne Street.

THE GENNINGS HOUSE, C. 1930. Victorian influences lost favor by the 1930s and many of the decorative details had been removed. Mrs. Gennings is standing by a wire fence, which replaced the original picket. (Courtesy of Dr. William B. Saxbe Jr., great-grandson of the Gennings.)

THE GENNINGS HOME, 2001. Some of the original lines of the house are still visible, but the period details have been lost to modernization.

The Dennis /Walker House, 2001.

The Dennis /Walker House (Built *c.* 1877) at 205 E. Wayne, 1960s. Italianate features such as the elongated windows framed by heavy carved limestone cornices, a two-story side bay, and low sloping hip roof define this two-story, brick home. At one time, a 20th-century porch replaced what was probably a narrow veranda with elaborate bracketed posts stretching across the front façade, as indicated by marks left on the brickwork. The outline of a second portico with bracketed posts is visible on the west side, where a second door with an ornate hood is located. The home was owned by Peter Dennis, who left it to his nephews, Fred and Joseph Dennis. Joseph, a local retailer and vice president of the State Savings Bank, converted it to the Maumee Hospital in the 1920s. Many Maumee residents were born in the maternity hospital, managed by Mrs. E.H. Wittebort. In the mid-1930s, the house was converted into a duplex. After Joe Dennis's death in 1944, the house became the property of a cousin, Mrs. Nellie Walker, whose two sons lived here with their families. The Robert Robinsons purchased the home from the Walkers in 1977 and returned it to single family living. Mr. and Mrs. Andrew Massey are the current owners.

George Morris Farmhouse (Built c. 1865) at 2006 River Road, c. 1900. The main block of this upright and wing farmhouse follows traditional patterns, with the exception of a few Victorian details such as the decorative wooden lintels and molding around the elongated windows. The back portion, with turned and bracketed posts on the narrow porch, may be a later addition. Original woodwork is found in the main block. The house was built by George Morris when he returned from service in the Civil War. Morris's farm extended between River Road and the Maumee River and was home to several generations of the Morris family. (Courtesy of Wilma Conyer.)

The Morris Farmhouse, 2002.

THE BROWN/HUDSON HOME, 2001.

THE BROWN/HUDSON HOME (BUILT C. 1877) AT 501 WEST BROADWAY, 1900. This simple, rectangular house is ornamented with Italianate details such as a 2-story, bracketed bay, the brackets under the gabled roof, and the decorative porch posts. The house was built by Thomas and Eva Brown. Mr. Brown, a millwright from Scotland, came to Maumee in 1859 to manage the Reynolds Flour Mill and later became a partner with Rueben Mitchell. He and his wife were active in the community. During the Civil War, Brown served his adopted country in the 130th Ohio Infantry. Later, he was elected to the Board of Education and as a Trustee of the Maumee Gas Co. After their deaths, the Brown's daughter, Nell, continued to live in the home and participate in the community activities such as the Women's Relief Corp and St. Paul's Episcopal Church. After Nell's death in 1951, the house became the property of Mrs. Helen Hudson. Current owners, Janet and Marc Adams, continue the restorations. (Courtesy of Janet Adams.)

THE PHILLIPS HOUSE I (BUILT C. 1882) AT 1215 RIVER ROAD, 2001. The Phillips family were early settlers of "Miami." Edward E. Phillips was born in 1861 near this site and lived in the small frame cottage at 1215, after his marriage to Margaret Evans in 1883. Edward was a successful builder and civic leader. He built the original portion of Fort Miami School as well as several homes in Miami Manor. He served six terms on Maumee Village Council and on other community boards. Sometime in the 1890s, he built this imposing brick home, relying on both traditional patterns and the newer contemporary "Four Square" designs. Phillips acquired extensive property between Ransom and Tappan Streets, and took great pride in his orchards along the latter. His grandson, Wallace, later remembered collecting peach pits with his grandfather during World War I to use in the manufacture of gas masks. His son, Ralph, superintendent of the Maumee Power Plant, lived at 1311 after the death of the elder Phillips. Interior features of the home include original wood-work and 10-foot ceilings. A graceful "wrap-around" Victorian porch blends in well. The cottage at 1215, later the home of grandson, Merlin Phillips, has been recently enlarged by the current owners, but the original house is still visible.

THE CLARK HOUSE (BUILT C. 1890S) AT 228 EAST WAYNE, 2001. This spacious Victorian home with gingerbread trim under the rambling front porch roof, railing with turned balusters and multi-gable roof was likely the scene of many social and civic activities. The home was built by Dr. and Mrs. Clark, who were quite active in community affairs. In 1898, the local newspaper reported that the Clarks were holding a "social" at their Wayne Street residence, the community band would make an appearance, and promised "good things to eat and drink." The occasion was a benefit for a John Wagner.

THE PHILLIPS HOUSE II, 2001.

THE "CARRIAGE HOUSE," 2002.

THE "CARRIAGE HOUSE" (BUILT *C.* 1870) AT 320 WEST BROADWAY, *C.* 1960S. (NRHP) According to local tradition, this charming home was once an outbuilding or carriage house, serving the Thatcher home on Cass Street. The sloping roof is similar to a saltbox, but with the main entranceway on the side. The first record of use as a residence is in 1885. In the 1930s, it was the home of Charles Charter, member of an old Maumee family. Fred Charter, his brother and proprietor of Charter Grocery (formerly Fredericks), lived directly across the street at 321 West Broadway in the family home (*c.* 1907). Charter-Cone American Legion Post was named in memory of William Charter. This home was purchased and renovated by Gordon Glann, also a member of a pioneer Maumee family, and his wife, Edna, in 1970.

John Schnapp House (Built c. 1887) at 216 East Williams street, 1960s. This upright and wing home has traveled around Maumee. Once located on Dudley Street, it was moved to 216 East William Street in 1921. The house was divided into two buildings at that time, placed side-by-side. Both buildings exhibited some Classic Revival details, particularly this unusual but handsome doorway flanked with wide molding and reeded pilasters supporting an ornamental cornice, indicating it may have been built at an earlier date. The house was owned by John Schnapp from 1930 until 1973. Schnapp added an indoor bathroom, a west wing, and a rear addition. In 1976, the house was scheduled for demolition to accommodate expansion of the Maumee Fire Station when it was purchased and moved by Dan and Claudia Stein to its present location.

210 West Dudley, 2001.

The Nelson/McCloud/Coyle House (Built c. 1870) at 208 East Dudlley, 2001. Decorative wooden lintels and trim around windows and entryway and a 2-story bay provide Italianate details to an otherwise simple frame home. The house originally located on the lot to the west, was moved to this site in 1915. A year earlier, the *Advance* noted that the "old Nelson property," which was once the "scene of lavish hospitality in the old day" where "some noted people have been entertained," had been vacant for three years, making its windows "targets for stones, snowballs and bean shooters." It was purchased by John Aigrisse, who planned to repair it for a rental. Mr. and Mrs. John McCloud purchased the home in 1966 and restored it to its original appearance. Current owners are the McCloud's daughter, Susan, and her husband, Michael Coyle, who continue to be stewards of their historic home.

The Johnson/McDonald/Smith House (Built c. 1868) at 421 West Broadway, 2001. (NRHP) This otherwise vernacular farmhouse is given an Italianate flair with the addition of brackets extending around the roofline and an ornamental hood over the upper windows in the gable end and above the projecting front bay, which separates the two wings. The front entranceway is framed by molding, and rounded panels in the door continue the Italianate effect. A small hooded bay on the east floods the stairwell with light and another bay projects from the upper floor. Piazza-style porches supported by heavily bracketed posts extend on either side. The house was built by Julia Dix Johnson, daughter of William Dix, and her husband, Peter, who operated the Pearl Mills until they closed in 1874. Justus and Minerva McDonald purchased the home in 1875. McDonald was a promoter and superintendent for the Narrow Gauge Railroad until 1880. That year he was elected Lucas County Commissioner and he held several other offices before his death in 1910. The home was later occupied by his daughter, Dolly, and her husband, Clarence Sager, and remained in the family until the mid 1930s. The house has been the residence of the Art Smith family since 1969.

The Pauken House (Built c. 1880) at 215 West Wayne, 1954. (NRHP) Mary Louise Pauken and neighbor, Judy Heilman, pose in front of the house, between the parking meters which lined Wayne Street when business leaders predicted (incorrectly) an expansion of the central business district in the post-World War II boom. (Courtesy of Marty Pauken.)

The Pauken House, 2001. The original block of this two-story, brick home may have once been embellished with brackets under the roofline and a smaller square entrance porch with decorative scrollwork, similar to the remaining rear porch. The round-headed windows with rounded hood molding are typical Italianate details. The front porch was added in 1917, when large verandas came into vogue. The Steven Pauken family purchased the house in 1910. Pauken was the proprietor of Pauken's Grocery on West Wayne Street. Groceries were delivered by horse-drawn wagon, and Mr. Pauken kept his horses ready in a barn at the rear of the property. His son, Paul, continued in the grocery business, and in 1933, after the death of his parents, Paul and his wife, Mary (Gay), reared their seven children here and the house remained in the family until 1996.

THE GANSLINE HOUSE, 2002.

THE GANSLINE HOUSE (BUILT *C.* 1889) AT 317 RIVER ROAD, *C.* 1900. In 1888, at the height of the "gas boom," a Maumee newsman commented that homes were "scarcer than hen's teeth." This modest, unembellished home, occupied by the Gansline family through the 1930s, is typical of countless houses built in Maumee in the late-19th century by local craftsmen to house a growing number of workers who found employment in the glass plant and related small industries. The front facade has been altered and the house enlarged, but the roofline and the original box shape are still visible.

The Rodd/McIntyre House (Built c. 1887) at 514 West Wayne, c. 1887. This interesting story-and-a-half with a central upright block, "lean to" additions on either side, and Victorian front porch with turned posts and brackets, has changed little over the years. At the time the early photo was taken, the house was owned by the Rodd family. In this unusual double exposure, Sue Rodd is seen in two different areas while the house remains the same. The east wing appears to be an open lean to. This was later the home of George McIntyre, who served four terms on Maumee City Council, including one as president, and was mayor of Maumee from 1953 until his death in 1960. Mrs. McIntyre continued to live in the family home until 1979.

The McIntyre House, 2001.

THE MILLER HOUSE, 2001.

THE GEORGE MILLER HOUSE (BUILT, C.1880S) AT 808 CORY STREET, C.1890S. This house is another example of a building that has been remodeled to meet the changing tastes of owners, although certain original features can still be seen. The window centered in the gabled end and the simple rooflines remain much the same, as do the two windows on the south facade. A picture window replaces the former doorway, which has been relocated at the far end of the porch. The chimney has also been relocated. A summer kitchen seen in the early photograph is gone. Also gone are the open fields behind the house where horses can be seen grazing. (Courtesy of Ruth Hoffman.)

Winslow/VanderHooven/ Westrick Home (Built c. 1892) at 220 West Wayne, c. 1900. (NRHP) Nearly every decorative element of the Victorian period is incorporated in this attractive home, which closely resembles early designs of George Barber's Cottage Souvenirs of 1890. These features include the original front entry porch with spandrels under the roofline, bracketed and turned posts and balustrades, and double doors leading into the front hall where a handsome staircase winds to the second floor. A second, flat-roofed porch on the opposite side with corbelled brackets, spandrels, heavily-turned posts, and balustrades is almost Eastlake in appearance. Matching 2-story gables on front and side are centered with double windows on the upper level and a triple-paned picture window with a small pane at top center. The elongated windows are framed with carpenter-style moldings, and a sunburst is centered in the rear gable. The house was originally fitted for gas lines for heat and light, and the original gaslights remain. Alida Winslow and her mother, Charlotte, were the first owner/occupants, and when Charlotte died in 1914, Alida converted the house to a duplex. The Heilman family purchased the home in 1935, and it remained a duplex until David and Ann (Heilman) VanderHooven returned it to a family home in 1965. Current owners, Dave and Nanci Westrick, continue to restore the home, bringing back the charm of the 1890s.

Winslow/VanderHooven/Westrick Home, 2001.

THE MORRIS HOUSE, 2001.

THE GEORGE MORRIS HOUSE (BUILT *C.* 1895) AT 817 PIERCE STREET, *C.* 1915. The Morris family is seen here relaxing on the front porch. The exterior of this late-Victorian cottage has remained relatively unchanged, although the large dormer across the front may be a later addition. This modest home with the unbroken roof slope, which extends over a broad porch running the full width of the house, is reminiscent of homes found in the southern areas of the state and is an unusual form in northwest Ohio. George Morris is the son of John Morris and the grandson of George Morris. (Courtesy of the Morris family.)

GENNINGS GROCERY (BUILT C. 1880S) AT 701 WEST WAYNE, C. 1912. Mr. and Mrs. Genning stand in front of their store. Harry Hennish was proprietor of a grocery store in this location in the late-19th and early-20th century until it was purchased by Fred Gennings, who continued in the grocery business until approximately 1920. A.J. Pfleghaar next moved his grocery business into the building and moved his family to the upper floor. The south wing may have been built at that time. In 1939, the *Advance Era* noted that Pfleghaar "will modernize" with "real brick veneer." Pfleghaar also installed the first full-plate glass front at that time. Many residents remember the building as the "La-Nan House of Beauty" in the 1960s. During the 1970s, the lower floor was home to Mad Anthony Books and the proprietors lived above.

HENNISH/GENNINGS/PFLEGHAAR GROCERY AND HOME, 2001.

THE BOTTE HOUSE, 2001.

THE BOTTE/HOFFMAN HOUSE AT 226 WEST WAYNE, *C*.1892. (NRHP) Simpler and smaller than its neighbor when built, this home has been doubled in size to meet the demands of family living. The original lines of the house, however, are clearly visible and the additions, including the wide wrap-around veranda with turned posts and balustrades are in keeping with the Victorian cottage design. Features such as windows and doors in the new portion are designed to match the original, which remain unaltered. This was the lifetime home of Leon Botte, who emigrated with his family from Belgium to Maumee in 1890 to become a glass blower in the Maumee glass plant. Later owners, Eric and Mary Hoffman, completed the expansion. Current owners, Scott and Trish Augustyniak, continue the stewardship of this vintage home.

Chapter 5
1900–1920

"The solidarity of American ideals depends very much upon the increase in the number of people owning their own homes."

House and Garden Book of Homes, 1920

The American Dream was visibly taking root in Maumee in the early-20th century as home ownership became more affordable and innovations in the building trades made it possible for every family to have their dream home—whether it be castle or cottage. The number of new building permits issued provided a source of pride in the *Maumee Advance Era*. Building contractors and carpenters such as Leo and Joseph Pauken, E.E. Phillips, and John Allmier could follow building plans available for a small fee in the latest home and garden magazines. Most new homes were smaller and more efficient than their Victorian predecessors and included such modern amenities as indoor plumbing and central heating! In addition, every style from the popular bungalow or cottage to a 10-room "mansion" could be purchased through the various mail order catalogues of Sears, Montgomery Ward, Palliser and Co., Aladdin, and the guru of craftsman movement, Gustaf Stickley.

MAUMEE RESIDENT R.R. ECKENRODE RELAXES IN HIS "CASTLE," SURROUNDED BY FURNISHINGS TYPICAL OF THE PERIOD, *C.* 1915.

431 East Broadway (built c. 1908). Plans for craftsman bungalows were readily available from such advocates as Gustaf Stickley and could be adapted by local builders, or the entire house could be purchased through a mail order company. This one-and-a-half-story bungalow with sloping hip roof and half-dormer is similar to a bungalow pattern, "The Dresdon," offered by Aladdin in the early 1900s.

Cannelli Inn (Built c. 1912) at 1503 River Road, 2001. The basic characteristics of the "California" Bungalow are the low, sweeping roof, wide veranda, and use of natural building material, such as the stone and slate used in this house. Floors are of pine, and walnut woodwork is found in the living room. This bungalow was built by John Canelli, who emigrated from Italy in 1900 and established a beer and wine importing and distributing business. During prohibition, the Canelli's enclosed the veranda and operated a "Spaghetti House," or as some speculated, a "Speakeasy." The current owners are Phil and Helen Kirk.

THE ECKENRODE AND BREISCH CALIFORNIA BUNGALOWS (BUILT 1915) AT 202 AND 204 EAST DUDLEY, 2001. (NRHP) Neighbors, Mrs. Leah Breisch Gibbs and Mrs. Samuel Eckenrode, first saw plans for a California bungalow in a house and garden magazine and shared their ideas with local architect, George Rheinfrank. The homes were unique with gray stucco walls and roofs extending fully over the wide porches. The interiors, with wood parquet and terrazzo floors, satisfied the popular desire to connect natural elements with the manmade environment. The California Bungalow was on the cutting edge of modern architecture and made fitting homes for the owners, who were major partners in the new State Savings Bank and proprietors of the American House Hotel. Eckenrode was also in the coal and ice business, a profitable endeavor in the early 1900s, before electric refrigerators and gas central heating were available to the average consumer.

MRS. BREISCH WITH HER DAUGHTER IN FRONT YARD OF 204 EAST DUDLEY, C. 1920. (Courtesy of Ed and Mary Goldberger, owners of 204.)

318 Kingsbury (Built c. 1902), 2001. One of the many styles to evolve toward the end of the century was the Queen Anne, characterized by turrets, towers, gables, and fanciful trim. The small circular window in the gable was a popular decorative element of the period. The houses on this page are modest Queen Anne adaptations, sometimes referred to as "Princess Anne," designed for middle-class homes. The house in the lower photograph was the home of Max Shepherst, an early director of the Toledo Metroparks, and his wife, Mildred, head librarian of the Local History Room of the Toledo-Lucas County Library. Both contributed immeasurably to the quality of life in Maumee and Toledo.

504 River Road (Built c. 1907), 2001.

211 East John (Built c. 1902), 2001. These two homes indicate that the Victorian cottage was still the choice of many for economy and ease of maintenance. With the introduction of modern machinery, carpenters could turn out fanciful and inexpensive cutwork. Even a simple one-and-a-half-story cottage could be up to date with the addition of fretwork and brackets, turned spindles, and delicate scrollwork for the gable end. The cutwork pictured here may have been replaced, but the cottages retain their original appearances. A larger, 2-story version of the rectangular Victorian cottage with a side porch and decorative trim can be seen at 332 East John Street.

604 River Road (Built c. 1912), 2001.

JULY 4, 1924, AT THE DONAVAN COTTAGE. The Donovans (far left and right) enjoy a summer afternoon with a friend on their front veranda. Sturdy rocking chairs and bamboo fans are nearby. (Courtesy of Marjorie Hutton, granddaughter of the Donovans.)

"THE COTTAGES" (BUILT *C.* 1910) AT 234, 232, 230 WEST DUDLEY, 2002. Referred to as "the cottages" by earlier owners, these three structures are examples of modest middle-class homes. The largest of the three, 234, boasts an especially spacious wrap-around veranda with a corner pediment. Turned spindles comprise the decorative row of bracketed and scalloped spandrels under the porch roof, and another row of turned balustrades and columns complete the gingerbread effect. Simply-carved, wooden fanlights are centered in the pedimented cross gables at front and sides, which are further embellished with fanciful trim. The adjacent 1-story house, for many years the home of George Didier, a native of France who immigrated to Maumee in 1898, is simpler in design. The home at 230 is a smaller version of 234 with the spandrels removed at one time from the front porch. The home at 234 was purchased by Mary Ann and Daniel Donavan in 1914, and the adjacent homes were presumably acquired at that time for rental property. The Donovans made this their home until 1931, and the properties remained in the family for many more years.

THE ROLLER HOUSE (BUILT 1911–1912) AT 432 EAST WAYNE. One of the most popular architectural styles of the late-19th and early-20th century was the quintessential American Four Square, which could be adapted to virtually any size, material, or budget. The house was what it implied—a square box with whatever embellishments the owners desired. This 2-story, brick home has all the stylistic details including a hipped roof, Tudor-type dormers with cross paned windows, and a large veranda across the nicely-balanced front facade. The lot was purchased in 1911 by Henry Roller, the proprietor of Roller's Saloon at the corner of East Wayne and Conant Streets, who soon began construction. An additional advantage of the Four Square was the economical use of space, which made it an affordable choice for family living. A typical example is a brick Four Square with multiple hipped dormers at 216 West Wayne, the family home of Louis and Mildred Hileman for over 40 years. Simpler examples are a group of three identical Four Squares at 125,127,and 129 West Broadway erected by Henry Hughes in 1911.

THE DENNIS/FOGEL HOUSE (BUILT c. 1912) AT 214 EAST DUDLEY, 2001. This Four Square home differs from most designs only in use of building material. The use of ornamental stone blocks as a building material became increasingly popular after the turn of the century, and many mail order companies such as Sears, offered plans for concrete block. Sears went a step further and provided machines for cutting the blocks, affording the customer, according to the catalogue, "a wonderful savings." Advocates noted that in addition to durability, stone or concrete were also fireproof. This home exhibits all the essential elements of the Four Square, with evenly balanced windows and tracery in the upper panes under the hip roof, and the broad porch with balustraded railings and graceful porch supports. Sylvester Dennis, commissioner of streets for 23 years, and his wife, Florence, made this their home for many years. The current owners are John and Janice Fogel.

The Bigley/Johnson House (Built c. 1907) at 212 East Wayne Street. A gambrel roof projecting from the upper floor is an unusual feature of this attractive Victorian home that incorporates several design elements. The circular window with decorative molding and the paired windows are often found in Queen Anne or Dutch Revival homes of the early-20th century. The wide veranda with balustraded railings and the one-story bay are popular features of the Victorian period. For many years, this was the home of C.P. Bigley, owner of Bigley's Hardware (formerly G.H. Blaker) at the corner of Conant and Dudley. Bigley was in the hardware business in Maumee for over 50 years.

The McCutchan/ Muenzer House (Built c. 1915) at 209 West Broadway, 2001. The use of multiple exterior materials provided another look to the Four Square. In May of 1915, the local newspaper announced that J.E. McCutchan, proprietor of McCuchan Dry Goods in the Union Deposit Building at Conant and Wayne, was preparing to build an 8-room home. The house was to be "shingled on the second story" and "built in modern fashion throughout." The contractor was Joseph Pauken, who expected to "produce one of the finest residences on the street." An almost identical home was built adjacent to the McCutchan residence and occupied by the John Shugars family. The Shugar's daughter, Leah Mack, wrote a popular newspaper column for several years. Although some additions have been made to the rear of the homes, they remain typical examples of the frame Four Square with third-floor dormers centered in the hip roofs and ample front porches supported by Tuscan columns.

Gambrel-Roofed Four Square (Built *c.* 1902) at 227 East Broadway. This home is an unusual variation of the Four Square with a Gambrel Roof and a recessed porch. The Gambrel roof was sometimes used to soften the lines of the Four Square and was said to provide additional space. The Gambrel often featured a decorative window in the gable end. Many homes of similar design can be found throughout Maumee. Joseph Riggles, Maumee's Commissioner of Building Inspection during the 1920s and 30s, purchased this home in 1915, when he moved his family from Toledo. It was one of the first "modern" homes built on East Broadway.

231 East Broadway (Built *c.* 1912), 2001. Another roof variation is the recessed arch or "horseshoe" gable on this Four Square house. The horseshoe roof was especially popular around the turn of the century and was adapted to various architectural styles, usually with a decorative window centered in the arch. For over 50 years, this was the home of Robert Corl, an engineer and well known artist and his wife, Marguerite, who had grown up at the Lucas County Children's Home where her grandparents were superintendent and matron. Marguerite, while a Sociology student at the University of Michigan, wrote a moving account of the challenges faced by the superintendent, staff, and residents at the Children's Home during those years.

THE COUCH HOME, 2002.

THE COUCH HOUSE (BUILT *c.* 1902) AT 134 EAST BROADWAY, 1960S. The Colonial Revival provided competition for the Four Square as the most popular building style of the early-20th century. This turn-of-the-century home employs some elements of the Colonial Revival but has undergone a few changes, including addition of the large, exterior chimney on the gable end. The front facade is nicely balanced with a classic doorway flanked by sidelights. Albert and Francis Couch renovated the home when they purchased it in 1941, and it was their family home for half a century.

A 1918 Advertisement for the Sherwood/Dussel House (Built 1915) at 122 River Road. This version of Colonial Revival is typical of those found in many small Midwestern towns in the early-20th century. A balanced facade, shingle siding, and white columns in the front entranceway create a traditional appearance. The house was featured in *House Beautiful Magazine* as an advertisement for central heating. The home was built by Dr. and Mrs. C.C. Sherwood along a curve on River Road, known as "Sherwood's Curve." After the road was moved, the sharp curve remained but much of the front yard was lost. Mrs. Sherwood was active in the community and was the first woman elected to public office in Maumee, serving several terms on the village council. The political connection continued with Cliff Dussel, who lived here until his death in 2000. Dussel served several terms on the Maumee City Council and was mayor of Maumee from 1961 to 1967. The home remains in the family.

Dr. C. C. Sherwood, Owner, Maumee, Ohio *Langdon & Hohly, Architects*
Heated and ventilated by a Kelsey Warm Air Generator

The Economy of Kelsey Health Heat

If we were to tell you how little coal the Kelsey Warm Air Generator consumed in heating a house of any given size, you would be inclined to think we were making extravagant claims.

But if you are interested, we shall be glad to tell you, not what we claim, but the experience of people who have used the Kelsey for years.

The Kelsey is unique in its system of circulating the hot gases on all four sides of its zig zag tubes, imparting so much of the heat to the fresh air that passes through them, that very little heat goes up the chimney. It goes where it belongs — into the house. In fact the smoke pipe is so cool that it can be touched with impunity.

Let us tell you how little it will cost you for fuel to keep your house cozy, filled with a constant supply of warm, fresh, humidified air, improving your health and decreasing your expense account.

New York
565-H Fifth Ave.

THE KELSEY
WARM AIR GENERATOR
(Trade Mark Registered)
306 James Street, Syracuse, N. Y.

Boston
403-H P. O. Sq. Bldg.

The Sherwood/Dussel House, 2002.

THE JOHN E. HANKISON HOUSE (BUILT C. 1913) AT 2902 RIVER ROAD. This attractive Colonial Revival home with its graceful columns supporting a pedimented porch incorporates many design trends advocated by the home decorating magazines in the early-20th century, including a dignified approach or entranceway, a sunroom or "breakfast porch," and a spacious, attached garage. (As automobiles became affordable for the middle class, the largest number of building permits issued in Maumee would be for construction of garages, a result of, according to the *Advance Era*, the increase in sales in the three new auto agencies.)

THE BOXELL/GUSSSES HOUSE (BUILT C. 1900) AT 2822 RIVER ROAD, 2001. In the spring of 1919, the *Advance Era* headline announced, "Values of River Frontage are increasing." But the move toward the river had already begun two decades earlier, when this handsome home was built in Sylvan Park, an early river front addition. The central block follows the Four Square form with the addition of a broad veranda and porte cochere. Toledo attorney, Earl Boxell, and his wife, Mary Alice, acquired the property in 1945 and it was their family home until the mid-1970s. The Boxells were active members of the community and often shared their home for special events.

Chapter 6
Going, Going, Gone

"They paved paradise and put up a parking lot. . . you don't know what you've got 'till it's gone."

Joni Mitchell, "Big Yellow Taxicab," 1970s

The message of this popular ballad rings as true today as when it was written. Too often we don't know the value of our architectural heritage until it's gone. When homes are removed from an historic district, whether for a parking lot or commercial development, the fabric of the neighborhood begins to unravel and soon it disappears altogether. Occasionally, homes such as the House of Four Pillars or the Forsyth House are brought back from the brink of demolition by someone with vision and an appreciation for our architectural past. The following examples are only a sample of those not so fortunate.

The Isaac Hull House (Built c. 1854) at 103 East Wayne. This predominately Greek Revival family home was built by Isaac Hull after his two daughters drowned in the Maumee River behind their E. Harrison Street home. The house remained in the family until it was razed in 1983. Over time, a Victorian bay and front porch were added and an addition was built on the west side. The house fell into disrepair in later years but retained its charm and continued to attract artists and architectural students. An ad hoc citizens group rallied to save the structure but were unsuccessful. The site is now a parking lot.

PARKING LOT AT THE CORNER OF CASS AND WEST WAYNE STREET.

THE SPANGLER HOME, 2002. This two-story frame home is thought to have been the home of Jacob and Ann Spangler, members of the first Methodist Class and hosts to Methodist Circuit Riders before the Methodist Church was built. The Spanglers celebrated their golden anniversary in their home in November, 1885. Although later converted to a three-family apartment building, the house retained it's Federal/ Greek Revival details, similar to the Forsyth House, including the front doorway with pilasters and pediment, and the narrow cornice under the roofline. When demolished in the early 1970s, bark covering the floor joists and rafters was still visible. It was replaced with an office building and parking lot.

THE WILCOX HOUSE (BUILT C. 1860S) AT 209 W WAYNE, 1960S. (NRHP) Even at the time of its demolition, this large, two-story, brick home still retained many architectural elements of the Victorian period, including the consoles under the roof and limestone cornices over the double hung windows. A one-story bay projected from the east side. The front entrance led into a winding walnut stairway with heavily turned newel posts. The floor joists were of solid walnut. The wrap-around porch was added in 1920. At the rear of the building, a large built-in oven was used for cooking in hot weather. This was the residence of John Wilcox, a local printer and publisher, community leader, Lucas County Commissioner, and president of the Lucas County Fair Board. Ruth Williamsen operated a tearoom here from 1937 through the mid-1950s, and the house was a popular place for special dinners and wedding receptions. During the 1960s, it was converted to apartments and offices. The house, and an adjacent century-old home, the Cassidy House, were demolished for a parking lot.

PARKING LOT AT ALLEN AND WAYNE, FORMER SITE OF WILCOX AND CASSIDY HOUSES.

THE COMSTOCK HOUSE (BUILT *c.* 1860S) AT 107 EAST WAYNE, 1960S. This handsome, square brick Victorian building was the home and office of Dr. R.W. Comstock, who practiced in Maumee for 35 years until his death in 1936. The family lived in the main portion of the house and Comstock's office was in the west wing. The small-town doctor making house calls in his horse-drawn rig was a familiar sight in the early 1900s. Converted to office space in the 1960s, the house was demolished for a parking lot a decade later..

THE COMSTOCK HITCHING POST AFTER IT WAS RELOCATED.

The McGovern/Mericle House (Built *c.* 1850s) at 113 E. Broadway, 1968. This handsome two-story frame residence, with Greek Revival details still evident at the time of its 2000 demolition, was the home of the McGovern family. George McGovern owned a livery stable on Conant Street and later converted his business to servicing automobiles. Horace P. McGovern, who resided here as late as 1930, was a village councilman and served as Mayor of Maumee in 1907. A decade later, the house was owned by George Mericle of the Koch Lumber Company. His sons, Herbert and Robert, also had positions with the company. In the 1930s, it was the home of Mac Mericle, a decorator, and his wife, Beatrice. In 1947, Mac was operating a Gulf Gas Station on the adjacent Conant Street lot. Sometime during the Mericle's ownership, the house was converted to a duplex. Residents recalled that the house still had original fireplaces and woodwork at the time of demolition.

117 East Broadway (Built *c.* 1880s). Next to the McGovern house sat the last remaining example of "stick style," a quintessential American architectural style characterized by vertical wood framing with intersecting gables and porches with diagonal braces. The vertical trim on the west gable was typical of the style. The house was converted to a duplex during the post-World War II housing shortage. It was demolished in 2001, along with the remaining two adjacent early-20th century homes, including an "arts and crafts" house. It was replaced by a parking lot.

Parking Lot.

The Reynolds/Alius/Mouen House (Built *c.* 1850) at West Wayne and Allen Streets, 1920s. A low-hipped roof with a wide cornice running below, six-over-six windows capped with stone lintels, and a classic doorway once distinguished this two-story brick building, which is similar in style to the St. Clair/Didier House directly behind it on West Broadway. It was built by George Reynolds, an early entrepreneur and civic leader. It became the home of Albert Alius, a prominent attorney, and his family until 1894, when it was purchased by Grafton B. Mouen, a local businessman. The Mouen family were the last residents before it was sold in 1935 to the Loesch Motor Company for commercial use. It was demolished in 1970 and the site was converted to offices.

The Reynolds House Shortly Before Demolition, 1968.

THE THATCHER/WOLFINGER HOUSE (BUILT *c.* 1830S) AT THE CORNER OF CASS AND WEST BROADWAY. The entranceway to this Greek Revival house was framed with pilasters and sidelights on both sides extending upwards to the five light transom and entablature. Narrow frame cornices extended over each window. In 1916, Charles Thatcher operated a convalescence home for women and children recovering from tuberculosis, still a potentially fatal disease in the early 20th century. The pure country air was believed to aid in their recovery. The house was later known as the Crippled Children's Home before the Lucas County Children's Home was built in 1890. It was razed in 1941, when the property was purchased for construction of a new home.

KALE HOUSE, 308 W. WAYNE. The entranceway to this Greek Revival frame house was similar to the Thatcher House, with a central entranceway framed with pilasters and side lights. The Victorian front porch was a later addition. The house was razed in the 1970s.

Glossary

Architrave	The lower part of a classical entablature that rests on the top of a column or pilaster, or sometimes the molding around a door.
Balluster	Supports for a railing, which is sometimes curved, sometimes straight.
Bracket	Usually decorative support under the eaves or overhangs, a popular element of Carpenter Gothic and late-Victorian architecture.
Clapboard	Boards with one edge wider than another that overlap on the outer wall of a frame structure.
Column	An upright shaft or pillar with a capital and base; it can be a major support or a decorative element, often used in Greek Revival architecture. Can be Tuscan (plain), Ionic, or Corinthian.
Console	Decorative ornament under the eaves.
Cornice	Refers to the upper section of an entablature or the ornamental molding that runs along the top of a wall or building.
Dentil	Small square blocks underneath an entablature or cornice.
Entablature	Comprises the architrave, frieze, and cornice in classical architecture, under the roof or at the top of a column. A distinguishing element of Greek Revival architecture.
Eyebrow Window	Small, often inward-opening windows under the eaves, often inserted into the cornice or entablature.
Fanlight Window	A semi-circular window, resembling a fan, often with tracery, over a door.
Fretwork	Ornamental openwork.
Finial	A curved and pointed ornament at the top of a gable or spire.
Fishscale	Decorative shingles of slate or wood which make a "fishscale" pattern.
Gable	The end-wall where a double pitched roof meets, forming a triangle.
Gambrel	A roof with two slopes, the lower being the steeper.

Greek Revival	An architectural style adapted to early-19thcentury architecture based on Greek Classicism, characterized by columns, pilasters, porticoes, and wide cornices and entablatures.
Hipped Roof	A roof with uniformly pitched sides and no gable.
Hood Molding	An ornamental element projecting molding over a window or door.
Italianate	Adapted from the Italian villa, the style is characterized by bracketed eaves and rounded arch windows, sometimes with hood mold, pendants, and finials and often a square, bracketed tower.
Lancet	A narrow, pointed, arched window found in Gothic architecture.
Lintel	A horizontal stone, brick, or wooden top piece of a window or doorway.
Mansard Roof	A tall roof with two slopes on all sides, sometimes encompassing a third floor. Often called a French roof.
Palladian Window	A three-section window with a central arched light and two rectangular lights (glass sections), named for its inventor, Andrea Palladio. It is a characteristic element of Georgian and Federal architecture.
Pediment	A triangular element used over doors, windows, and porticoes.
Pilaster	Designed to resemble a column, the pilaster is a slightly projecting pillar, often decorated with carved fluting or "reeded," and sometimes topped with a classical order. Often found in Greek Revival architecture.
Portico	A porch, sometimes with a pedimented roof supported by columns. A double Portico is a two-story porch with columns and pediment.
Return	A term referring to a right angle turn in a molding or cornice.
Saltbox	A gabled-roof house with a steep rear slope to the roof, originating with the practice of adding a "lean-to" on the rear of the building. The name refers to the shape of a Colonial saltbox. In some areas of the country, particularly the Midwest, it is referred to as a "cat slide."
Sidelights	Small glass panes flanking a doorway.
Spindle	A decorative, turned, wooden shaft used in stair railings and porch trim, particularly popular during the Victorian Era.
Transom	A window composed of small panes over a doorway.
Turret	A small tower found in Italianate (usually square) and Queen Anne (usually round) homes that resemble their larger counterparts found in European castles and villas.

SUGGESTED READING

For Further Reading on American Architecture

Asher, Benjamin, *The Builders Companion,* Dover Publications, originally published 1827, reprint (1969).

Bicknell, A.J., *Bicknell's Victorian Buildings,* Dover Publishing, Fifth edition, originally published 1878, reprint (1979).

Chambers, Allen, Poppeliers, John C., and Swartz, Nancy B., editors, *What Style Is It?,* National Trust For Historic Preservation, (1983).

Comer, Lee and Ligibel, Ted, editors, *Lights Along the River,* Landmarks Committee of the Maumee Valley Historical Society (1983).

Frary, I.T., *Early Homes of Ohio,* Dover Publications (1970).

Grow, Lawrence, *More Classic Old House Plans,* Main Street Press, (1986).

Kitchen, Judith, *Old Building Owner's Manual,* Ohio Historical Society (1983).

Tunnard, Christopher and Reed, Henry Hope, *American Skyline,* Houghton Mifflin Company, T Printing (1956).

Varney, Almon C,. *Our Homes and Their Adornment,* J.C. Chilton and Co., (1882).

Wendler, Marilyn, *Foot of the Rapids: Biography of a River Town, Maumee, Ohio, 1838–1988,* Daring Publishing (1988).

———, *Images of America: Maumee, Ohio,* Arcadia, (2000).

Williams, Henry L and Ottalie K., *A Guide to Old American Houses, 1700–1900* A. S. Barnes(1962).

Wright, Richardson, editor, *The House and Garden Book of Houses,* Conde Nast and Co.,1920.